PARENTS ARE TEACHERS
A Child Management Program

Wesley C. Becker, Ph.D.
Department of Special Education
College of Education
University of Oregon
Eugene, Oregon

RESEARCH PRESS
2612 NORTH MATTIS AVENUE
CHAMPAIGN, ILLINOIS 61820

PARENTS ARE TEACHERS

A Child Management Program

Thirteenth printing 1980

ISBN   0-87822-019-4

Designer: PAM BLAIR THOMPSON
Editor: SHERREL HISSONG

To My Parents

WILLIAM HENRY BECKER, SR.

&

ALCEY MAE COLE BECKER

*For the teachings they gave their eleven
children with love and dedication.*

Contents

Introduction

PARENTS ARE TEACHERS has been designed to help parents learn to be more effective teachers of their children. The program is based on the latest knowledge of teaching methods growing out of the science of behavior. The program shows parents how to systematically use consequences to teach children in positive ways what children need to learn to become effective people.

Experimental versions of this program have been used in many ways. In Project Follow Through, a sequel to Head Start, many disadvantaged parents have been taught to be more effective teachers of their children by working through the program under the direction of a group leader. (Group Leader Guide may be obtained from the publisher at $2.00 per copy.)

Because the vocabulary has been kept as uncomplicated as possible, the program should be of considerable value to *teacher aides* in poverty area programs as well as to parents. When technical terms or unusual words have been needed, they have been defined at the bottom of the page on which they appear.

Another group for whom this program has been found to be valuable are parents of children with special problems. *Clinical psychologists* have served as group leaders with parents of children showing behavior problems and have used this program to teach parents how to eliminate the problems which brought them to the clinic. *School social workers, elementary guidance counselors,* and *special education teachers* have used the program with a variety of special children whose problems have made it necessary that their parents systematically aid the teachers in training them.

Finally, we have found the experimental version of this program to be extremely helpful to the *average parent* seeking to do a better job. Why children (or adults for that matter) do what they do is not quite the mystery the romanticists would like us to believe. There are general principles or laws of behavior. The principles describe the procedures by which behaviors can be changed in specified ways. When a parent or teacher knows

1

about these procedures, she or he knows what to do to teach children new behaviors. The most common report given to us from parents is that this training program helps them to become more positive and loving in interacting with their children. Shouting, yelling, and griping are replaced by clear instructions and positive consequences.

WESLEY C. BECKER
September, 1970
Eugene, Oregon

How to use this program

1. Read a unit. Use the definitions when you find words you do not know.

2. Do the exercises for that unit, writing in the answers.

3. Correct your exercises using the answers provided at the back of the book. You may correct one page at a time or just at the end of the exercise.

4. Begin any projects related to the unit you are on.

5a. For those meeting with a group leader, do only one unit between each group session.

  b. For those doing the program on their own, do no more than one unit a day. Use the projects to work on various changes you would like to make in yourself or your child. Be sure to keep records of the behaviors you are working on. This is important in evaluating changes and in reminding yourself of what you are about.

6. Keep in mind that *knowing* is not *doing*. Shoot for changes in what you do as well as in what you think and say.

Unit 1

CONSEQUENCES: REINFORCERS AND PUNISHERS

People teach each other how to behave

Gwen doesn't say anything about it until they are seated in the booth. She is ready to burst, holding her new success in until they are away from the rest of the office staff and by themselves.

GWEN: Guess what? I asked for a raise! I asked for a raise!

MARGE: Did you get it?

GWEN: I think so. He suggested ten dollars. I said, "How about twenty dollars?" And he said he would check it with Jordan, but he thought it was o.k. That's $240 a year more.

MARGE: That's great. But I thought you didn't care about money.

GWEN: Jimmy and I might find some way to use it. [*Pause*] Let me buy your lunch to celebrate and sort of say thanks for your help.

MARGE: Sure, I'd like that too. [*Their sandwiches come and they begin to eat lunch quietly.*]

GWEN: Marge, I was thinking about some of the things that happened to me this morning getting up. The floor was cold so I quickly reached for my bathrobe and slippers. I bumped into a doorway and got hurt, so I looked more carefully at the next doorway. Then I got frozen in a cold shower and had to turn it off and warm it up before starting again. You know, I've never paid attention to things like that before, but the series of incidents keeps saying to me "your surroundings control* you." I'm not sure I like that.

MARGE: It's a good thing you're not a Polar Eskimo*.

GWEN: How's that?

MARGE: Can you imagine living in an environment* where the average winter temperature is minus forty degrees? That exerts a considerable control over you.

GWEN: How do you know so much? You seem to be the well-spring of knowledge today.

MARGE: I've been reading a paperback about the Polar Eskimos. Almost everything they do is guided by the battle to survive starvation and coldness. They have little privacy 'cause it is impractical to heat a house more than fifteen feet in diameter. It's too cold to bathe. It's sometimes necessary to kill dogs they need and love, if hunting is poor and there is nothing else to eat. Often families are isolated from each other for months at a time while searching for food.

GWEN: I wouldn't like that at all. When you look at it that way, we really have a friendly environment, even at thirty-one degrees on a March morning.

MARGE: Gwen, you said that you didn't like the idea of your surroundings controlling you. But you know they do, whether you like it or not, just as they do for Eskimos, sailors, desert Arabs, or jungle dwellers.

GWEN: [Agreeing] You're right. But isn't it funny that we usually don't think it controls us?

---

control: To influence your behavior.

Polar Eskimo: Member of a group of people living near the North Pole.

environment: Your surroundings. The world you live in. The events and things around you which influence your behavior and physical condition.

6

MARGE: That's usually because we have *learned* to live with our environment. It has taught us how to survive in it with a minimum of punishment. It's only when we get hurt by it that we really pay attention. Just look at all the things people do to avoid being hurt by their environment. We make buildings, beds, air conditioners, food storage facilities, heaters, and so on. You might say that nowadays we build the environment that controls us.

GWEN: [*She really liked that idea.*] We build the environment that controls us . . . We do it in ways that make us happier. I don't think I mind being controlled by an environment that I can help control. That doesn't sound so bad.

MARGE: You're silly, Gwen. It makes no difference whether you mind or not. That's the way it is.

GWEN: Marge, when we left our coffee break this morning, you said something about how we make each other what we are by the way we react to each other. Like I teach Reggie to be inconsiderate and my boss to take advantage of me. Is that really true?

MARGE: Gwen, you just agreed with the idea when you said "we build the environment that controls us."

GWEN: [*Still puzzled*] Well, that's different, isn't it?

MARGE: The principle* is the same. We do what we are taught to do, whether by other people or by the physical environment. We do more of the things that are nice or fun, and do less of the things that hurt us. That's all. If we can provide the right kind of consequences* for each other's behavior,* we ought to be able to make

---

principle: A general rule.

consequences: Events which follow a response which can strengthen or weaken such responses. Rewards, punishments.

behavior: What we do. Responses.

---

each other happier people. [*Marge's thoughts flashed back to Kansas University and the long discussions she had with her psychology* instructor about changing people.*]

GWEN: I think it would be fun to try to build a world with happier people. Hey, we better get back to work. It's almost one o'clock.

GWEN: [*Crossing the street*] Well, I did one thing about the environment that controls me today.

MARGE: What's that?

GWEN: I got it to give me a twenty dollar raise. [*They both laugh and go inside.*]

---

psychology: The science of behavior.

People learn how to behave from each other

- Parents teach children.

- Children teach parents.

- Husbands teach wives.

- Wives teach husbands.

- All behavior is taught.

You can be a teacher too

- You can change behaviors in others that need changing.

- You can help others change your behavior.

- You can change your child's behavior.

Did you ever wonder why we train people for almost every important job in society except the most important of all?

Mothers and fathers have a difficult job, but few are trained for it with the teaching skills they need.

In this course, we hope to provide you with some important teaching skills.

See what Peter's mother learned . . .

Mother changes Peter (and Mother)

Peter is a four-year-old boy.[1] His mother was having great difficulty managing him and sought help. Peter often kicked objects or people, removed or tore his clothing, spoke rudely to people, bothered his younger sister, made various threats, hit himself, and was easily angered. He demanded constant attention. He had been seen at a clinic and was found to have poor verbal skills. He was said to be very active and possibly brain-damaged.

Peter's behavior was observed in the home an hour a day for sixteen days. During an hour Peter showed from 25 to 112 behaviors objectionable to his mother. These included kicking people or objects, removing or tearing his clothes, speaking rudely, hurting his younger sister, making threats, hitting himself, getting angry, and the like. When Peter misbehaved Mother would often attend to him and try to explain why he should not do so and so. At times she would try to interest him in some new activity by offering toys or food. Mother would sometimes punish Peter by taking away a toy or misused object, but Peter was usually able to persuade Mother to return the item almost immediately. At times he was placed on a chair for short periods of time as a punishment. Lots of tantrum behavior usually followed such discipline. Mother responded with additional arguments, attempting to persuade Peter to stop.

Peter's behavior was changed by the following procedure. An observer in the home would cue Mother by raising one, two, or three fingers. One finger was raised when Peter showed an objectionable behavior. Mother was instructed that this meant that she was to tell Peter to stop what he was doing (a warning signal). If Peter did not stop, two fingers were raised. This meant that Mother was to immediately place Peter in his room and shut the door (punishment for Peter). He had to stay there until he was quiet for a short period before he could come out. If Peter was playing in a nice way, three fingers were raised. This meant that Mother was to go to Peter, give him attention, praise him, and be physically affectionate (reinforcement).

Peter's objectionable behavior dropped to near zero within a few days. Follow-up observations showed a continuing good interaction between Peter and his mother and an absence of the objectionable behaviors. Peter was receiving more affection from his mother and approaching his mother in more affectionate ways. Mother was much more sure of herself, provided clear

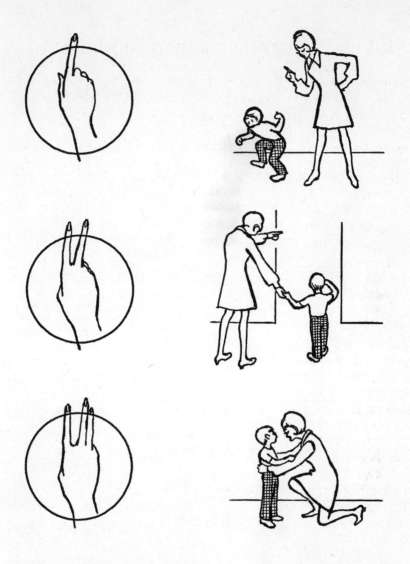

consequences for Peter's behavior, and no longer gave in after starting a correction procedure.

Peter's mother learned that by following good behavior from Peter with attention and affection, and by consistently giving a mild punishment for objectionable behavior when a warning failed, Peter's behavior changed dramatically.

Peter's mother learned that she had to consistently respond to behaviors she wanted to strengthen with positive reactions. YOU CAN LEARN TO DO THIS TOO (if you don't already, that is).

In the next example, Mrs. E. finds out that she does not need to use punishment at all to teach children to be better behaved in the classroom . . .

A teacher learns to manage an uncontrolled classroom of first graders

Observations on February 1: "Six children were in a reading group and fifteen were working on individual projects. The noise level for the entire classroom was extremely high and went higher just before recess. Some behaviors noted included whistling, running around the room (five occasions), yelling at another child (many times), loud incessant talk, hitting each other in recess line. Mrs. E. would re-establish quiet by counting to ten after giving a threat."

Mrs. E. was a young teacher who had not been taught how to manage children. She attempted to control the children by shouting and scolding, but it would only slow down the unwanted behaviors for a short time, and she would have to "get on them" again. Figure 1 shows the percent of time two of her children were showing behaviors incompatible* with working and paying attention.

Edward was six years and eight months old and of average ability. His teacher described Edward as distractable, with poor attention and poor work habits. He was not able to comprehend what he read. He never finished assignments. He was often seen wandering about the room or turning in his seat. He made quite a few odd noises with his mouth. He was in speech therapy and was being seen by the social worker.

Elmer was two months older than Edward and was also of average intelligence. He apparently started out the school year working well, but got worse. He was described as nervous and very active. He would not work. He cried or had a tantrum if his work was criticized. Observers thought Elmer might be brain injured since he was so very active. He did not stay in one place on any task very long.

---

incompatible behaviors: Can't do them both at the same time. You can't sleep and run. You can't be cooperative and aggressive at the same time.

TECHNIQUE FOR CHANGE

The behavior of most of the children in the classroom was changed beginning with the sixth week of the study (Figure 1, page 14) by having the teacher follow three procedures:

1. *Clear signals.* Make your rules clear so that the children know what is expected of them. Repeat rules as necessary.

2. *Ignore disruptive behaviors.* Do not attend to the behaviors you wish to weaken*. Get involved with other children showing behaviors you wish to strengthen*. Praise a child showing behavior incompatible with disruptive behaviors.

3. *Praise* the children for improvement in behavior. *Catch the children being good,* rather than bad. Tell them what it is that you like that they're doing. Award privileges to those showing good behavior. For example, say "You can lead the salute because you are paying attention so well."

THE RESULT

Prior to week six this teacher used very little praise. After week six, over 90% of her comments to children were positive rather than critical. Elmer and Edward changed greatly, as did the teacher and other members of the class. It took some time for the teacher to become comfortable in her new role of being a "reinforcer" for the children, but the children responded to her new behavior *whether she felt comfortable about it or not.* The classroom became quieter; many members learned to work on tasks for long periods of time. There was order and cooperation. The teacher found she had more time to teach now that she spent less time trying to *control* the children.

The above classroom is just one of many where large changes have occurred when the consequences for children's behavior have been changed. In a follow-up to this study, it was found that just repeating rules was not effective in changing behavior in the classroom. Only when *praise* was given for following the rules, and disruptive behavior was *ignored,* were results similar to those in Figure 1 obtained.

---

weaken: To decrease the rate at which a behavior occurs.

strengthen: To increase the rate at which a behavior occurs.

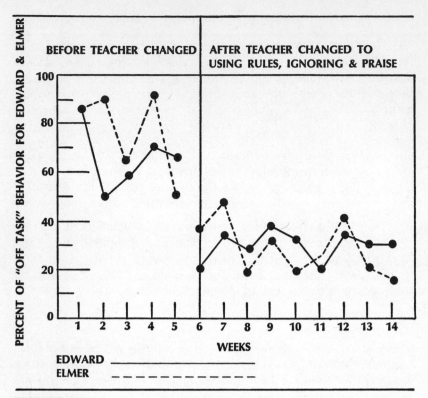

FIGURE 1

Percentage of *off task* behavior for two children in Class E, before and after change in teacher's behavior.[2]

Consequences strengthen
or weaken behaviors

Research on teaching has convincingly demonstrated that there are events which occur *following* behaviors (consequences) which function to strengthen or weaken behaviors. Events *following* behaviors which strengthen behaviors we call *reinforcers.* Events *following* behaviors which weaken behaviors we call *punishers.* No longer following a behavior with a reinforcer also weakens behavior. Which consequent events strengthen or weaken behavior is determined by investigation. Generally, events we would label as rewards, or the stopping of painful events, have been found to strengthen the behavior they follow.

In the case of Peter, his appropriate behaviors were reinforced by attention, praise, and physical contact. Peter's objectionable behaviors were punished by placing Peter in his room if he did not comply. He was "shut off" from possible reinforcement for a period of time to punish an objectionable behavior. In Mrs. E's class, praise was the main reinforcing consequence used by the teacher to increase on task behavior. Disruptive behaviors were weakened by ignoring them. That is, the teacher no longer followed disruptive behaviors with attention (the reinforcer for such behavior).

Summary

Rules about consequences
1. *Follow responses you wish to strengthen with reinforcing events.*
2. *Follow responses you wish to weaken with punishing events.*
3. *Withholding all forms of reinforcement for a specified time period is a useful form of punishment.*
4. *Responses can be weakened by no longer reinforcing them.*

Generally avoid the use of punishment. Problems can be created when punishment is used in the wrong way. We shall learn more about effective punishment later. For now, focus on the use of rewards to influence your child.

NOTES TO UNIT 1

[1] R.P. Hawkins, R.F. Peterson, E. Schweid, and S.W. Bijou, "Behavior Therapy in the Home: Amelioration of Problem Parent-Child with the Parent in a Therapeutic Role," *Journal of Experimental Child Psychology,* IV (1966), 99-107.

[2] W.C. Becker, C.H. Madsen, C.R. Arnold, and D.R. Thomas, "The Contingent Use of Teacher Attention and Praise in Reducing Classroom Behavior Problems," *Journal of Special Education,* I (Third issue, 1967), 287-307.

Unit 1 • Exercise 1

These exercises are designed to help you learn more readily the new concepts covered in the unit. You are to write one word in each blank. You may go back through the unit as much as you wish in deciding which words are right.

1. The events and things around you which influence your behavior and physical conditions are called the en_____ (see page 6).

2. A principle is a general r_____ (see page 7).

3. Events which follow a response which can strengthen or weaken responses are called c_____ (see page 7).

4. Behaviors which cannot be performed at the same time are called _____ behaviors (see page 12).

5. Consequent events which maintain or strengthen responses are called _____ (see page 14).

6. Punishing events are also consequences, but they _____ responses, rather than strengthen them (see page 14).

7. At lunch Gwen presented the conclusion that "Your surroundings _____ you." Marge replied with the example about the Polar Eskimos (see page 6).

8. We change our behaviors to survive in a given environment with a minimum of _____ (see page 7).

9. Men make buildings, beds, air conditioners, food storage facilities, heaters, etc. in order to avoid being hurt by their _____ (see page 7).

(You are on your own now.)

10. In many ways, we build the environment that _____ us.

11. When we are working on building our physical environment, we almost always attempt to change it in ways that will make us _____.

12. The same principle can apply to our social en-_____. Other people control many of the things we do. However, if the things we do don't make us happy, then we can try to change our social environment by t_____ other people different ways to respond to us.

13. Peter was thought to be very active and possibly brain-_____.

14. Peter's mother would try to divert him from objectionable behaviors by offering him _____, _____, and access to other activities. She may actually have been reinforcing his bad behavior.

15. Sometimes Peter's mother attempted to _____ him by taking away a toy or placing him on a chair for a short period of time.

16. When Peter was punished he frequently exhibited much _____ behavior to which his mother responded with additional arguments and attention.

17. Mother's attention might be expected to _____ tantrum behavior.

18. We would expect Peter's behavior to change if the consequent events were changed. Therefore, if reinforcement for undesirable behavior was removed and reinforcement for desirable behavior was begun, we would expect an increase in _____ behavior.

19. The procedure used with Peter was, first, to have Mother _____ Peter when he showed an objectionable behavior; second, if he did not stop, he was to be placed in his room and the door shut; third, if Peter was playing in a nice way, his mother was to give him attention, praise, and _____ _____.

20. The result of these procedures was that Peter's _____ behavior dropped to near zero within a few days.

21. Mrs. E. was a teacher of _____ grade children.

22. These children were observed to run around the room, yell, talk loudly, hit other children, push, etc. The teacher would attempt to establish _____ by counting to ten after giving the class a warning.

23. The teacher's major means of keeping control was by _____ and/or scolding.

24. Shouting and scolding slowed down unwanted behaviors for only a _____ time.

25. Figure 1 shows that prior to a change in teacher behavior Edward and Elmer were spending approximately _____ per cent of their time showing behaviors incompatible with working and paying attention.

26. Observers thought Elmer might be brain injured "because" he was so _____.

27. The teacher followed three procedures to change the _____ of her students.

28. She made her _____ clear, so that the children knew what they were supposed to do.

29. She _____ disruptive behaviors and thereby removed a source of reinforcement from them.

30. She also _____ the children for improvements in their behavior.

31. Using this procedure, you might say she was trying to "catch them being_____ rather than bad."

32. Thus the three key words for the procedures the teacher used would be rules, praise, and _____.

33. In a follow-up study it was found that just repeating the _____ was not effective in changing behavior in the classroom. Praise for on-task behavior and ignoring off-task behavior had to be used also.

34. Research on teaching has shown that consequent events can function to _____ or weaken responses.

35. Consequent events which weaken behaviors are called

_____.

36. Consequent events which strengthen behaviors are called

_____.

37. Behavior may also be weakened by no longer following it

with a _____.

38. When we weaken behavior by not reinforcing it, we simply

make a rule (and stick to it) that previously

_____ consequences of a response will

no longer occur.

39. A "rule-of-thumb" about _____ is that

they usually are the same sort of events that we call rewards.

RULES ABOUT CONSEQUENCES

40. Follow responses you wish to _____ with

reinforcing events.

41. Follow responses you wish to weaken with

_____ events.

42. Withholding all forms of reinforcement for a specified

time is a useful form of _____.

43. Responses can be weakened by no longer

_____ them.

*Check your answers in the back of the book. Where you have
made errors, study the unit again.*

Unit 2
KINDS OF REINFORCERS AND PUNISHERS

In Unit 1 we saw that reinforcers can be used to strengthen behaviors and punishers to weaken behavior. This unit is aimed at helping you identify reinforcers and punishers, and at teaching a rule about how to create new reinforcers and punishers.

Unlearned* reinforcers and punishers

Unlearned reinforcers include such things as food, candy, toys, water, warmth, activity, and the like. Events such as these will usually strengthen behaviors they follow without having to be paired with an effective reinforcer.

Unlearned punishers include such events as loud noises, pain-producing events, excessive heat or cold, and the like. Unpleasant events such as these will usually weaken behaviors they follow without having to be associated with an effective punisher first.

Learned reinforcers and punishers

Events which at first have no effect on behavior can become reinforcers and punishers.

Praise from parents like "good job," "that's pretty good" *become reinforcers* for most children if they are closely followed

---

unlearned: Not learned. No training required for it to happen.

---

in time by other "good things" (food, warmth, affection, special privileges, fun activities).

Similarly, words like "No," "Don't," "Stop that" *become punishers* if they are closely followed by a slap on the wrist, a spanking, or loss of privileges. For Peter, mother's warning ("Stop that") quickly became an effective punisher. "Stop that" was followed by being placed in his room and became a signal that punishment would occur if the warning was not followed. Learned reinforcers and punishers are established through training.

> **RULE: To make some event (such as praise, a checkmark on a chart, or money) a reinforcer, closely follow in time such events with effective reinforcers.**

Examples of the rule

To teach children the "value of money" we might give a young boy two cents to buy bubble gum at the store and have him exchange the two cents for the bubble gum with the grocer. Money is closely followed in time with chewing bubble gum. Later you might be able to use money as a reward at home for doing a good job.

To teach children to respond to praise, Mother might tell Joe after he picked up his room, "You did a good job in cleaning your room. I'm pleased. I'm going to make your favorite dessert tonight." Words of praise are followed by something special Mother knows will please Joe.

Sarah's mother decided to use pieces of red paper cut into squares as rewards for Sarah being cooperative and not fighting. When Mother would see Sarah playing nicely with Julie, she would just walk over and give Sarah a piece of red paper and smile. Mother told Sarah that if she got five red papers by noon, she would get an ice cream bar with lunch. Later, Mother had Sarah mark on a chart how many papers she earned each day, and gave her a reward only on Friday night. The red papers were at first closely followed by a reward. Later, the red papers led to points on a chart, and finally to a reward on Friday. Mother taught Sarah to work for red papers and points on a chart.

SOCIAL REINFORCERS

Two types of learned reinforcers are especially important to the parent. *Social* reinforcers involve the *parent's behavior*— her tone of voice, words of praise, giving attention, smiling, touching, and being near. Most teaching by parents is based on the use of social reinforcers as the immediate* consequence for good behavior. For example, Mother says *"Thank you,"* when Aaron brings in the mail. Or, "You did a *good job;* you tied your shoes." . . . "That's a *big boy;* you stopped crying." . . . "Get ready for bed and I'll *read you a story."* . . . *"I'm proud of* your work in school." In each of these examples, the italicized words from mother are attempts to reinforce desired behaviors.

TOKEN REINFORCERS

Token reinforcers are another kind of learned reinforcer. They consist of such things as points, stars, Green Stamps, and poker chips which have been made reinforcing through being paired with other reinforcers.

Money is a very important token reinforcer in our society. We can exchange money for a variety of reinforcers. The money by itself is useless. It is only when it is made a basis for obtaining other reinforcers that it has value to us.

Poker chips quickly acquire value for the gambler. S & H Green Stamps become valuable to the housewife who finds they can be traded for things she wants.

Similarly, we can make a variety of objects token reinforcers for children and use them to motivate children to do things. The brass ring on the merry-go-round, tickets, bottle caps, and bubble gum cards have at various times been token reinforcers. Token reinforcers consist of *things* which are given to people. They can be collected, saved, and usually exchanged for other reinforcers.

It is very useful for a parent to know how to use token reinforcers and social reinforcers in teaching her children behaviors necessary for group living.

There is still another kind of reinforcer you can use. . .

---

immediate: Happens right now. The reinforcer must occur *immediately* after a response to be effective.

23

GRANDMA'S RULE

The following are examples of Grandma's Rule. See if you can figure it out.

"You can play ball when you finish your homework."

"When everybody is seated at the table and quiet, father will say Grace and we can eat."

"Eat your vegetables and then you can have some pie."

"When your room is picked up, I've got a special treat for you."

"Take your bath and then you can have some cookies and milk."

"You can go out and play after you take out the trash."

The next two examples are NOT examples of Grandma's Rule.

"You can go and play if you'll do your homework later." "Sure, Mom."

"You can go to the movies tonight, if you'll do your homework tomorrow."

GRANDMA'S RULE

You do what I want you to do, before you get to do what you want to do.

First you work, then you play.

To teach a child to carry out his responsibilities, require the less preferred* activity to come before a more preferred activity (fun).

Activities a child likes to do can be used to REINFORCE doing things a child cares less about.

ACTIVITIES CAN BE USED AS REINFORCERS.

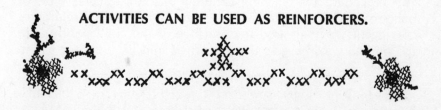

---

preferred: Will choose over other possibilities when given a choice.

JUSTIN'S MOTHER LEARNS TO USE GRANDMA'S RULE

At first, Mother told Justin, "You didn't make your bed so you can't go out and play." Justin pouted all day and still did not make his bed. He said, "Why should I? I can't go out and play anyway." He also complained that Mother never hugged or kissed him. They were constantly battling.

Justin's mother then heard about Grandma's Rule and the importance of reinforcers. She told Justin, "When you make your bed, you can go out and play." Justin lit up. "You mean I can go out if I make my bed? Yippie!" The bed was made in two minutes and Mother was able to praise and hug Justin for doing a good job.

Justin's mother was so taken with the change in Justin that she decided to learn more about child management* and the use of rewards.

ACTIVITY REINFORCERS

If any preferred behavior can be used to reward less preferred behavior, then we are able to find out what is reinforcing for any child *by watching what he chooses to do*. One psychologist observed that the four preschool children he wanted to teach to read spent most of their classroom time "running and screaming." So he made a rule. "Sit and listen for two minutes, and I'll let you run and scream." Gradually, he required longer sitting, listening, and working for less running and screaming. They were a hard working group of children in no time, and well behaved.

A general procedure for using reinforcers

The procedure for teaching children that a particular type of behavior leads to an effective reinforcer is to make the reinforcer contingent upon* desired performance. *If* the child performs in the desired way, he gets the pay-off; *if not,* he does not get it.

---

child management: Good ways of teaching children what you want them to learn.

contingent upon: Depend upon. When the reinforcer is given depends upon when the response occurs. The reinforcer has been made contingent upon the occurrence of the response.

After the child has learned to work for a particular pay-off, it is possible to teach the child to work for other pay-offs simply by treating a new pay-off as if it were as much fun as other reinforcers he knows about. "If you do this job, I'm going to let you work your arithmetic sheet. How about that?" This approach is similar to the one Tom Sawyer used to convince his friends that whitewashing a fence was the supreme reinforcing activity.

Summary

1. Events can be made reinforcers by closely following them with effective reinforcers. We teach children to respond to praise by pairing praise with food, warmth, and other reinforcers.
2. Events can be made punishers by pairing them with effective punishers. "No" followed closely by a hand slap can quickly teach the two-year-old to stop reaching for the lamp when his mother says "No."
3. Three groups of reinforcers important to a mother are social reinforcers, token reinforcers, and activity reinforcers.
    A. Social reinforcers involve the parent's behavior— words of praise, attention, smiles, nearness.
    B. Token reinforcers are things which can be exchanged for other reinforcers such as money, poker chips, points, and gold stars.
    C. Activity reinforcers are behaviors children like to perform when given a chance. These might include running, games, art activities, singing, eating.
4. Grandma's Rule says any behavior which a child will engage in can be used to reinforce behaviors which a child will not readily engage in. You simply require that the less preferred activity be performed before the more preferred activity is allowed.
5. The general procedure in using reinforcers is to make the reinforcer contingent upon the occurrence of the desired response. If the correct behavior occurs, the reinforcer is given; if the correct behavior does not occur, the reinforcer is not given.

Unit 2 • Exercise 1

Write one word in each blank. Go back to the unit as often as you need to find the correct answers.

1. Reinforcers can be used to strengthen behaviors and punishers to _____ behavior.

2. Unlearned reinforcers and punishers do not require previous _____ to be effective.

3. Food, candy, toys, and warmth are _____ reinforcers for most people.

4. Loud noises, pain-producing events, and excessive heat or cold are unlearned _____ for most persons.

5. Events can be made reinforcers by closely _____ them with effective reinforcers.

6. Money can be made a reinforcer if money can be exchanged for other _____.

7. By consistently following "stop that" with placing Peter in his room if he failed to stop, Peter's mother made "stop that" a learned _____ for Peter.

8. Words of praise can be made reinforcers by closely following them with other _____ such as food.

9. Pieces of red paper can be made reinforcers by showing Sarah that they can be _____ for things she wants.

10. Social reinforcers involve the b—————————— of people (praise, smiles, attention, nearness).

11. "Thank you," "Good job," "Great" are examples of —————————— reinforcers.

12. Token reinforcers consist of t—————————— such as points, gold stars, money, and poker chips.

13. For many housewives, S & H Green Stamps have become —————————— reinforcers.

14. Green Stamps are token reinforcers rather than social reinforcers because they are —————————— which can be —————————— for other reinforcers.

15. The following (is/is not) an example of Grandma's Rule: "You can play ball if you will do the dishes when you get back."

16. The following (is/is not) an example of Grandma's Rule: "Be dressed by 7:30 and I will drive you to school."

17. Grandma's Rule requires that a less preferred activity be performed —————————— a more preferred activity can occur.

18. We can tell what is likely to be reinforcing for a given child by w—————————— what he likes to do when given some freedom.

19. Reinforcers must be made contingent upon responses to be strengthened. This means that if the correct behavior occurs, the —————————— is given; if the correct behavior does not occur, the reinforcer is —————————— given.

20. Preferred activities can be used to strengthen

_____ preferred activities.

21. If Reginald laughs when Mickey makes funny faces, and Mickey starts making funny faces more often, Reginald's laughing is a _____ reinforcer.

22. Laughing is a social reinforcer because it involves the

_____ of a person and serves to strengthen

making funny faces.

23. Put an X on the one that is not a social reinforcer: (a) "good" (spoken), (b) a smile, (c) a gold star, (d) a pat on the back.

24. Put an X on the one that is not a token reinforcer: (a) Green Stamps, (b) money, (c) points, (d) praise.

25. A learned reinforcer based on parent's behavior is called a

_____ reinforcer.

26. Token reinforcers can be collected and used as a medium of exchange for other _____.

27. Examples of _____ _____

are money (i.e., ye olde paycheck), points, stars, Green Stamps.

28. Examples of _____ _____

are words of praise, smiling, being near, a pat on the back.

29. Grandma's Rule is based on the idea that generally any behavior which a child will readily engage in can be used to reinforce any _____ of lesser strength.

30. Grandma's Rule is very important to the parent because the parent needs only to _____ what her child frequently does to find out what is a _____ activity for the child.

31. Establishing a contingency would be like setting up a rule that if, and only if, the child performs a desired behavior will he get a particular _____.

32. The _____ use of reinforcers means that if the child performs in the desired way he gets the reinforcer; if not, he does not get it.

Check your answers with those in the back of the book. Where you have made errors, study the unit again.

Unit 2 • Exercise 2

IDENTIFYING CLASSES OF
POTENTIAL REINFORCERS

Suppose you are a child and each of the following events occurs following your behavior and functions as a reinforcer for you. Indicate what kind of reinforcer each event would be. Write *S* before each example of a social reinforcer, *T* before each example of a token reinforcer, *U* before each example of an unlearned reinforcer, and *A* before each reinforcing activity or privilege.

1._____ Someone says, "You're pretty smart."

2._____ You get to play house.

3._____ Check marks are placed on a card (exchange for a toy later).

4._____ You are given food.

5._____ You're chosen for running errands at school.

6._____ Someone winks at you.

7._____ You are given M & M's.

8._____ The grocer gives you Green Stamps.

9._____ You get to play outside.

10._____ Someone says, "You make me happy."

11._____ You are given raisins.

12._____ You win poker chips.

13._____ You get some popcorn.

14._____ You choose the game at recess.

15._____ You are given money.

16._____ The group cheers you.

17._____ Someone smiles at you.

18._____ Mommy reads to you.

19._____ You get to fly a new kite

20._____ You are given candy

21._____ You get to go to the zoo.

22._____ You get hugged.

23._____ You are given lemon drops.

24._____ You get to play with a model airplane.

25._____ You get to play a game.

26._____ Someone pats you.

27._____ He touches you.

28._____ She looks at you.

29._____ You get to work a puzzle.

30._____ You get some peanuts.

31._____ You get to play with a balloon.

32._____ You are given animal crackers.

33._____ Someone kisses you.

Check your answers with those in the back of the book. Where you have made errors, study the unit again.

Unit 2 • Exercise 3
DESCRIBING A BEHAVIOR
TO STRENGTHEN OR WEAKEN

Describe below a behavior you would like to *strengthen* in your child. Be sure to write about something you can see or hear that your child does.

_____

_____

_____

_____

_____

_____

Describe below a behavior you would like to *weaken* in your child.

_____

_____

_____

_____

_____

_____

If working with a group leader, bring this to your next group session. If working alone, refer to this later when deciding on a behavior change project.

Unit 3
WHEN TO REINFORCE

There are three rules about when-to-reinforce which are important for parents:
1. In teaching new tasks, reinforce immediately rather than permitting a delay between the response and reinforcement.
2. In the early stages of learning a task, reinforce every correct response. As the behavior becomes stronger, require more and more correct responses before reinforcing (gradually shift to unpredictable* intermittent* reinforcement).
3. Reinforce improvement* or steps in the right direction. Do not insist on perfect performance on the first try.

RULE 1

Reinforce immediately

MOTHER TRAINS KAREN TO DAWDLE
Karen was "learning" to get herself ready for school. At first Mother would call her in the morning, Karen would get up, and Mother would dress her. It was faster for Mother that way. Karen received lots of attention and did not have to do much herself. Mother decided she had had enough of that nonsense

---

unpredictable:	You can't tell when it will occur.
intermittent:	It occurs now and then.
unpredictable intermittent:	Something that occurs now and then, but you can't tell just when.
improvement:	Getting better.

---

and told Karen it was her job to get ready. Mother went to work on breakfast.

Karen put on her socks and panties and just sat on the bed. Mother soon checked and found Karen just waiting. She nagged and scolded. "Karen, what am I going to do with you? You'll be late for school. Now hurry up and get ready."

Five minutes later Karen had still not appeared for breakfast. Mother checked Karen again and again and found little progress. Her slip was on, but Karen was looking at one of her picture books. Again Mother nagged. "Karen, come on, hurry up. You'll be late. Do I have to treat you like a baby?"

Karen's mother was making several mistakes. Let's list them:

1. She withdrew all attention and help for getting dressed from Karen at once.
2. When Karen was put on her own, Mother gave attention only to the dawdling. Not once did Mother praise Karen for getting herself partly dressed. What received immediate attention from her mother was *not getting dressed*. Getting dressed was given no attention.

It should not be surprising to learn that within three weeks, Karen had trained her mother to nag at her from the time she got up to the time she left for school, usually late. Mother had trained Karen to dawdle*.

LISA'S MOTHER DOES IT THE RIGHT WAY
Lisa's mother faced a similar task of helping her five-year-old to learn to get ready for school by herself. She too had over-babied Lisa by doing many things for Lisa that Lisa could have done by herself. When she realized the time had come, however, she approached it quite differently than Karen's mother.

First she told Lisa it was time for her to do more things for herself. The night before, she reminded Lisa about what she was to wear tomorrow, and together they set her clothes out where she could easily find them. When Mother woke Lisa in the morning Mother gave her a hug, and said, "Let's see how far you can get dressing yourself while I put the coffee on. I'll be right back to check." Lisa's mother was back within a minute and noted that Lisa already had her panties and slip on. She immediately commented on this. "You really know how to dress yourself. That

---

dawdle: Fool around or do nothing.

36

really pleases me. You're a *big* girl." Lisa worked harder to please Mother and obtain attention from Mother by being a big girl. Lisa was not taught to dawdle as Karen was.

WHAT IS LEARNED IS WHAT IS REINFORCED
We teach others how to behave by what we reinforce. If reinforcement does not immediately follow the response we want to strengthen, it becomes possible that some other response might be reinforced. By the time Karen's mother gave her attention, she was no longer getting dressed. *Not getting dressed* was being reinforced by mother's nagging attention. Any delay in reinforcement* increases the chances that wrong behaviors will be taught.

At this point, a mother of four children may protest, "But I can't be with all my children at the same time and reward everything I want them to learn immediately." Of course not. Immediate reinforcement is very desirable, but there are ways to get around it when it is not possible.

OVERCOMING THE DELAY WITH WORDS
For children who understand language, it is usually possible to bridge a delay period by using words. The thing to do is simply tell the child exactly what he or she did that pleases you. If Karen's mother had simply focused on the fact that Karen had her socks and panties on the first time she came back, and *ignored** the dawdling, very likely Karen would have been dressed by the second time her mother came back.

LEARNED REINFORCERS AND DELAY OF REINFORCEMENT
The principle of immediacy applies to *any reinforcer,* learned or unlearned. Most of the time parents use praise or other social reinforcers as the immediate reinforcers. Now and then, the social reinforcers are paired with a special treat, a hug, or whatever, to keep them important. Social reinforcers such as "You're right," "That's good," "I like that," are easy to give immediately and are always at hand. When praise doesn't work, then we must learn ways to make praise important for children. This problem is discussed in the next unit.

---

delay in reinforcement: Time occurs between the response and the reward.

ignored: Paid no attention to.

RULE 2

Early in learning, reinforce every response. Later, reinforce some of the responses.

A positive consequence* after every right response early in the game helps the child learn what you want. Lisa's mother was sure to reinforce each right response (putting on her panties and slip) on that very first day. Later Lisa's mother might simply have to comment on how pretty she looks today to help maintain* good dressing behavior by Lisa. This version of Rule 2 may be easier to remember:

> To get it going, reward every time.

> To keep it going, reward intermittently.

As parents we are most concerned about teaching our children behaviors which will continue when we are no longer there to reward them. We want the *behaviors* to persist in the absence of direct rewards from us.

There are some very definite ways in which persistent behaviors can be built. Did you ever notice how persistent the behavior of a gambler can be? Even though the odds are against him, and he loses every time, he keeps playing and playing and playing. Now and then he wins a little or a lot. But he can never tell whether he is going to win (get reinforced) or not. Games of chance generally involve unpredictable intermittent reinforcement for the players. To teach persistence, the trick is to start by reinforcing nearly every response early in the game, and then to slowly reinforce less and less in an unpredictable way.

MOTHER TEACHES JEFF TO WORK ONLY WITH HER
Let's consider two approaches to getting Jeff to do his homework. In the first case, Jeff is told to do his homework, and Mother stays near by working in the kitchen.

---

positive consequence: Reinforcer. Reward.

maintain: Keep it going. Get it to persist.

Jeff just stares at his arithmetic exercise until Mother comes over and says "What's the matter, Jeff?" Mother knows he can do the work, because when she helps, he does do the problems.

"I can't get this one."

Mother says, "Go ahead and try, I'll watch."

Slowly he writes down the correct answer and Mother praises him. "See you can do it. Now go ahead and work the rest."

When Mother busies herself with other things, Jeff goes back to staring in the air.

When Mother checks back, Jeff appears to be busy and says, "Help me with this one."

And so it goes. Every single problem is done only when Mother is there giving attention. Jeff has been taught not to work unless Mother is there although Mother did not intend this.

MOTHER TEACHES JEFF TO WORK ON HIS OWN

Let's contrast this with another procedure. A colored card with ten squares on it is placed on the desk where Jeff works. Jeff is told that if he is working when Mother checks on him, Jeff will get to mark off one of the squares. When ten squares are filled, he can have an ice cream bar (or a soft drink, etc.).

Jeff is expected to do thirty minutes of homework each day. Mother uses a kitchen timer which makes a soft ding when it goes off. When the timer dings, Mother looks to see if Jeff is working. If he is, she tells him to mark a square. Mother sets the clock first for thirty seconds, then one minute, then twenty seconds, then three minutes, then two minutes, then ten seconds, then four minutes, then one minute, then five minutes, then three minutes, etc. An unpredictable set of times is used, and they slowly get longer and longer. Jeff can't predict when the bell will go off. To keep from losing points he has to keep working.

As the time intervals are increased, he is taught to work longer and longer on his own. After Jeff can work for thirty minutes easily, the points are dropped, and Mother just checks on a now-and-then basis.

Good habits such as brushing teeth, dressing, cleanliness, and balanced eating are built by using Rule 2. Just remember that when your child is first learning the good habit, he must be rewarded *every* time he brushes his teeth or dresses himself completely, etc. Then later, to keep him following these habits, reward him *occasionally*.

RULE 3

Reward improvement

One of the troubles with the school system which gives grades according to a standard level* of performance* is that those who know the most to begin with usually get the most reinforcement. Under such conditions, the students who know less to begin with are reinforced less for trying than those who start out knowing more. The teacher defeats her own objectives with this kind of grading. Those who need to learn the most are reinforced the least, and thus are likely to "learn" less. This problem can be overcome if teachers focus on rewarding improvement.

Parents also need to be sensitive to signs of improvement. Reinforcers should be given for *getting better*. Catch your child getting better and praise him for this behavior. Do not insist on perfection right off. Remember also that what is a big step for one child may just be a small step for another.

To apply this rule in teaching a child to work on his own, we first praise the child for completing short tasks, and gradually lengthen the tasks.

Another way to think about this point is to reward your child for trying. If he works hard at tying his shoes and fails, still tell him you are pleased to see him try. "If you keep trying, you will get it."

Do not reinforce the wrong behaviors:

If a behavior is reinforced only now and then, it follows from what we know about intermittent reinforcement that such behaviors are likely to be persistent.

---

standard level:	A fixed level of performance is required, such as 90% or higher to get an A grade. The shoes must be tied so they won't come off, or no reward for tying your shoes.
performance:	Behavior. What you do.

40

If tantrums by Jerome are usually punished but sometimes he gets his parents to "give in," we might guess that they would become quite persistent.

We can accidentally train our children into bad habits by occasionally giving in, even though we "know better." To change an undesirable behavior, the parents must be VERY CONSISTENT in not rewarding that behavior.

Summary

1. Immediate reinforcement is most effective. Delays can be overcome by telling your child what he did that you liked.
2. To get it going, reward every time. To keep it going, reward intermittently.
3. Reward improvement.
4. Be careful not to now and then reward undesired behaviors.

Unit 3 • Exercise 1

Fill in the blank with the correct word. You may refer to the unit as often as you find necessary.

1. In teaching a new task, it is best to reinforce

   i_____ rather than allowing a delay.

2. To be most effective, do not permit a _____

   between response and reinforcement.

3. Immediate consequences are more effective than

   _____ consequences.

4. In the early stages of learning a task, _____

   every correct response.

5. After the behavior becomes stronger you should require

   _____ correct responses before you rein-

   force.

6. Gradually shift from reinforcing every correct response to

   reinforcing only _____ of the responses.

7. Karen's mother gave Karen attention only when Karen was

   _____ getting dressed.

8. Karen trained Mother to _____.

9. Mother trained Karen to _____.

10. By the time Karen's mother gave her attention, she was no

    longer getting _____.

11. Not getting dressed was being reinforced by Mother's nag-

    ging _____.

12. Any delay in reinforcement increases the chances that _____ behaviors will be taught.

13. Lisa's mother prepared her to begin dressing herself by t_____ about it the night before and laying out her clothes.

14. In the morning Lisa's mother checked her progress o_____.

15. Lisa was _____ for her progress in dressing herself.

16. We teach others how to behave by what we _____.

17. Lisa worked hard to please Mother and receive _____ from Mother.

18. A delay in reinforcement can be bridged by t_____ your child what you are praising him for.

19. The principle of immediacy applies to _____ reinforcer, learned or unlearned.

20. It is easy to give _____ reinforcers. They are always at hand.

21. To get it going, reward _____ time.

22. To keep it going, reward _____.

23. Reinforcing every response gets new behavior going _____.

24. Reinforcing intermittently helps to keep behaviors going (makes them p_____).

25. The gambler cannot tell if he will win or not. Reinforcement is un―――――――――――― as well as intermittent.

26. Games of chance generally involve unpredictable ―――――――――――― reinforcement.

27. Persistence is taught by slowly shifting from reinforcing all the time to reinforcing less and less in an ―――――――――――― way.

28. In the first example, Jeff's mother was reinforcing Jeff's doing homework only when she was ――――――――――――.

29. Jeff was taught to do homework on his own by making reinforcement from Mother ――――――――――――.

30. Mother set a timer for variable times which slowly got longer and ――――――――――――.

31. To keep from losing ―――――――――――― Jeff had to keep working.

32. When Jeff earned ten points, his card could be exchanged for an ―――――――― ―――――――― ――――――――.

33. After Jeff worked for thirty minutes easily, the ―――――――――――― were dropped and Mother just checked now and then to p―――――――――――― his good work.

34. Parents need to be sensitive to signs of ――――――――――――.

35. Reinforcers should be given for getting ――――――――――――.

36. When rewards are given only for high performances, the children who need the ―――――――――――― the most get the least.

37. Another way of thinking about rewarding improvement is to reward your child for _____.

38. We can accidentally train our children into

_____ _____ by occasionally "giving in" when a child misbehaves.

39. To change an undesirable behavior, parents must be very _____ in not rewarding that behavior.

Check your answers with those in the back of the book. Where you have made errors, study the unit again.

Unit 3 • Exercise 2

RECORDING NOTES ABOUT A BEHAVIOR TO BE CHANGED A WEEK FROM NOW

1. Describe your target behavior in observable terms:

    _____

    _____

2. Provide a daily report, as follows:

DAY	HOW OFTEN DID IT OCCUR TODAY?	WHAT DID YOU DO ABOUT IT? *(For this week, try to deal with it as you would have before starting this course.)*
1.		
2.		
3.		
4.		
5.		
6.		
7.		

Unit 4
USING STRONGER REINFORCERS

Some children have not been taught to respond to praise from adults.

Some children have not been taught to like school work, homework, or any kind of work.

Some children don't care. They are turned off by people and their world.

How does this happen?

What can we do to make them care?

Most children who do not care are children who do not receive many rewards or reinforcers. A day is mostly one punishing experience after another. *Large* changes are easily produced in such children simply by switching from the use of criticism and punishment to the use of praise and other reinforcers.

Teresa stops complaining about Mother and school

Mother came to the clinic with Teresa because she seemed emotionally upset. She complained about having to go to school. She would not do the chores around the house without griping. Quite often she would go into a rage and run to her room when Mother asked her to do things. At school she was said to be withdrawn and would not complete her work. She didn't like her teacher. She complained about being slapped by her teacher during the first week of school. Mother didn't know quite what to do. Mother was truly concerned and so was Teresa's father.

After discussing the situation with Teresa's parents and a visit to school by the counselor, a reward system was designed to help Teresa. Instead of being punished, shouted at, criticized, and slapped, Teresa could earn points each day on the chart. On Saturday, the money she received was determined by the number of points she earned that week.

AT SCHOOL TERESA EARNED POINTS FOR:

Class participation in reading	1 point daily
Class participation in arithmetic	1 point daily
Completion of assignment in reading	1 point daily
Completion of assignment in arithmetic	1 point daily
Pleasant social behavior	1 point daily

AT HOME TERESA EARNED POINTS FOR:

Doing dishes Mon., Wed., and Sat. evening	2 points each
Making her bed	1 point daily
Cleaning her room on Saturday	4 points
Being pleasant with her mother and father	2 points daily
Special requests from her mother	2-10 points

Teresa's teacher would send a note home each day indicating how many points she had earned and how she had earned them.

Teresa and her mother made a chart at home that looked like this one:

TERESA'S PROGRESS CHART														
HOW TO EARN POINTS:	S	M	T	W	T	F	S	S	M	T	W	T	F	S
SCHOOL POINTS	X	5	5	5	4	5	X	X	5	5	5	5	5	X
DISHES	X	2	X	2	X	X	0	X	2	X	2	X	X	2
BED	1	1	0	1	1	1	1	1	0	1	1	1	1	1
CLEAN ROOM	X	X	X	X	X	X	4	X	X	X	X	X	X	4
BEING PLEASANT	0	2	1	0	2	2	2	1	2	2	2	2	2	2
SPECIAL REQUESTS	X	X	X	3	X	X	X	2	X	X	X	5	X	X
DAILY TOTALS	1	10	6	11	7	8	7	3	10	8	10	13	8	9
WEEKLY TOTALS	50							61						

You can see from the chart the points Teresa earned during the first two weeks. Her mother was quite amazed at the change in Teresa. She didn't seem like the same girl. She was much happier, quit complaining about school, and received good reports from her teacher each day.

At first Teresa's mother doubted whether it was right to use money to reward Teresa. It seemed wrong to her. Teresa should just do those things without a reward. But we explained that Teresa was not doing what Mother wanted and that she needed help to learn to do them. After the two weeks of success Teresa's mother had no doubts that she was doing the right thing. Both she and Teresa were so much happier. Mother decided it was really worthwhile to focus on the positive and to use rewards instead of punishments.

Overcoming school failure with token reinforcement systems

Many children have been taught that school work means failure and punishment. They skip school and drop out. School has not paid off for them. When children have been exposed to such failure, the use of strong, obvious, and immediate reinforcers for each response may be necessary, along with teaching programs which permit success. Token reinforcement systems are one practical way to introduce stronger reinforcers in the classroom or the home.

The rules for planning a token system may be stated as follows:

1. Start with tokens which can be quickly and easily given.
2. Tokens are *learned reinforcers* which can be traded for other reinforcers. A variety* of payoffs increases the chances that you have a reinforcer for most children.
3. Reinforce a lot in the beginning and gradually reinforce less as the behavior improves.
4. To get off the system, so you won't need it forever, tokens should be paired with praise and affection so that these social reinforcers will gain reinforcing power.

---

variety: Many different kinds.

Tokens have been used successfully where other approaches have failed. The following examples show the power of special reinforcers.

An after school program for potential dropouts

Wolf, Giles, and Hall[1] studied sixteen pupils from two elementary schools located in the low income district of Kansas City. The children worked in a remedial* teaching program during the summer and after school hours during the regular school year. Comparisons were made with a group that went to the regular school and was not involved in a remedial program.

The token reinforcement system was somewhat like a trading stamp plan. The students had cards marked off into squares. The cards were checked by an instructor whenever a student had earned a point. *Each checked square was a token.* When a child first joined the program, points were given for each problem which was worked correctly. As the child did better, the amount and difficulty of the work required to earn points increased. The number of points given to a child for a particular bit of work was determined by the instructor alone or by bargaining with the child.

Filled pages of points could be exchanged for a variety of goods and events, such as a circus, swimming, zoo, daily snacks, candy, soap, novelties; or long-range goals, such as clothes or second-hand bicycles. A number of other contingencies* were provided in the program. In some instances, favorite subjects or popular activities could be attempted only after completion of work in less favored areas. A bonus was given for attendance. Improvement in grades led to a party after each grading period for all students who had improved. The students also received

---

remedial: One that corrects the problems.

contingencies: Reinforcers (or punishers) given contingently; that is, given only when a certain behavior happens.

---

bonus points for reports of good behavior from their regular class teacher.

During each of the prior two years the median gain* by the remedial groups on an achievement test* had been .6 years. The gain during the year of the token group was 1.5 years. Comments by the regular school teachers suggest that the remedial program benefited the regular classroom as well. Not only were the program children helped, but their increased participation and changed attitudes increased the achievement of other children in the classrooms.

An in-school program
for an adjustment class

Most of the early studies of token programs have used at least one adult for each four or five children. O'Leary and Becker successfully devised a token program which could be used by one teacher with a classroom of seventeen problem children. The children had been placed in a special class because they were behavior problems and behind in classwork. They were from disadvantaged homes. The children were nine-year-olds working at a beginning first-grade level.

Eight of the children averaged seventy-six per cent off task behavior* before the token system was started. The teacher had a most difficult time carrying out any procedures which might be considered teaching. She would usually leave the classroom worn out. The token program was in effect from 12:30 p.m. to 2:00 p.m. each day.

---

median gain: The gain made by the middle person in the group, when gains are ordered from high to low.

achievement test: A test of reading, arithmetic, and other language skills. The test provides scores in terms of grade levels. Each year the average child should gain one year (1.0) on the test.

off task behavior: In this case, it includes being out of seat, talking out of turn, making noises with objects, talking to peers when it is not permitted, turning away from one's work, and so on. Behaviors that do not involve paying attention to teacher or working at a school task.

On the first day of the token program, the class rules were placed on the blackboard and the token procedures explained to the children. Small ten-cent notebooks were taped to each child's desk. The children were told that they would receive points in their notebooks each 15 minutes. At each period they could get from one to ten points. A mark of ten meant that they were following the rules very well, while a mark of one indicated that they were not doing their tasks.

The points could be traded for small prizes, such as candy, comics, perfume, and kites. A variety of items was provided to increase the chances that at least one of the items would be a reinforcer for each child.

At first, the tokens were traded in at the end of the token period. Step by step, the children were required to work up to four days before trading tokens and the points required for a prize were increased.

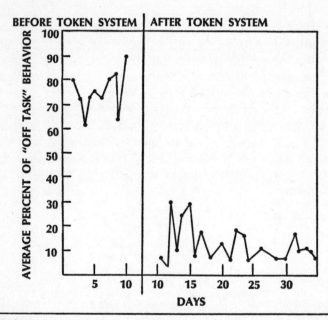

FIGURE 2

Average percent *off task* behavior during base and token periods for eight children.[2]

The results are summarized in Figure 2. Before tokens, the children averaged seventy-six per cent off task behavior. This dropped to ten per cent during the token period. It was now possible to begin to teach. The children quickly learned to respond to the teacher's praise which was paired with the giving of points. The class became the best behaved class in the school. Before, it was the worst. The children learned to tolerate delays in trading tokens for prizes. Reports indicated that the children also behaved better in other classroom activities when points were not given, and during music and library. The rewards for the programs cost $86.76 during the eight weeks it was in effect. Rewards appear to be less expensive than psychologists! Eighty dollars would pay for only three hours of a psychologist's time.

Informal token systems

Many of us working with teachers and parents on a day-to-day basis have had to devise reinforcement systems for single children. Here are some procedures we have tried and found to work:

1. Jimmy was aggressive and did not complete class assignments. The teacher worked out a procedure with his mother. Jimmy brought a note home each day he worked hard and was cooperative. With a note Jimmy could watch TV for a specified period that evening. Without a note he could not. The note was a token or ticket earned for good classroom behavior which could be traded for the privilege of doing something Jimmy liked to do at home.
2. Aaron was a fourth grade boy. He would not get down to work in class, preferring to mess around or play with his friends. He was often reported to be aggressive with younger children coming to and from school. Aaron earned check marks on the board, one check for each ten minutes of good working behavior. If he earned ten checks, he could spend thirty minutes in the kindergarten supervising younger boys in the use of carpentry tools. The younger children could use the tools only when he was there. They liked him to come. Aaron learned to work in the classroom, and work cooperatively with younger children.
3. The problem was how to reduce the fighting among her

four boys. Mrs. James solved it by having a family meeting where she suggested that each of the boys could earn "tickets" (pieces of colored paper which they cut themselves). She would carry the tickets in her apron pocket and give them out every so often when she saw the boys were playing nicely. She tried to give between five and ten to each boy each day if he earned it.

She watched them when they were in the yard as well as in the house. When she gave tickets, she praised the boys and told them what she *saw them doing* that she liked.

"Ken, you helped your young brother get dressed. That's being cooperative." She gave him a blue ticket.

"Tom, when you and Ken play together like that on the floor with that card game it pleases me to see you treat each other so nicely." She gave Ken one of his blue tickets, and Tom a green ticket.

Each week the family decided between them what tickets could be traded for. The first week, twenty-five tickets were traded for a Saturday movie. Each ten beyond that was good for five cents spending money at the movie. The second week, they planned a trip to the zoo. It took twenty tickets to get to go, with the rest of the tickets to be traded for spending money as before.

Mrs. James reported that giving tickets *helped her to remember to praise* her boys for cooperating, instead of always scolding them after they got into a fight.

4. Lynn sucked her thumb. Mother set up a chart so that Lynn could earn three check marks a day, one before school, one after school, and one after dinner, if no thumbsucking occurred. Each twenty points earned could be exchanged for a ticket to a ride at Kiddie Amusement Park. After the first week showed progress, Mother had Lynn's teacher send home a daily note worth two more points, one for the morning and one for the afternoon. The procedure helped Lynn to remember about her thumb, and she was not sucking it at all two months later.

"WHY THAT'S BRIBERY"

On the first look, the use of rewards with children is sometimes confused with bribery. What is the difference? Bribery refers to one of two things. With adults, we talk about bribery where someone is paid to do something illegal. We certainly are not talking about that.

With children, bribery usually refers to the situation where the child *will not do something* and the parent says, "Okay, Mary, I'll give you a dime if you'll do the dishes." Mary was supposed to do something. When she failed to do it, her mother "upped the ante" to get her to do it. *That is bribery.* It is not a good procedure because Mary is being *rewarded for not doing* what she is supposed to do.

The use of rewards as we have proposed here involves setting up the conditions beforehand. "For these behaviors, you can get these payoffs. For those behaviors, you get those payoffs." The children are awarded the payoff if it is earned, and not awarded it if it is not earned. If the terms are right, the children will do what we want them to and get rewarded for it. If the terms are wrong, we will have to revise them, *but not while the child is misbehaving.*

Summary

Turned off children are unmotivated* children. They can become motivated by rewarding them for the things we want them to learn to do.

There has to be an effective payoff for behavior if the behavior is to persist.

We need to reduce or eliminate the use of punishment, except under special conditions to be covered later. We need to increase our use of effective reinforcers.

When praise, attention, and affection do not work as reinforcers, then we have to go back to more basic unlearned reinforcers such as food or fun activities.

A variety of approaches to using token reinforcers have been discussed in this unit. Our goal is to get you thinking about the many ways you might be able to set up special reinforcement systems when they appear to be needed.

---

unmotivated: Do not want to do things usually expected of children.

The key to token systems is to:
1. *have some tokens which are easily given (paper, points, poker chips, marks, pennies, marbles),*
2. *which can be traded for a variety of rewards or rewarding activities.*
3. *Remember to reinforce a lot in the beginning, and gradually reinforce less.*
4. *Finally, remember to praise when you give out tokens.*

NOTES TO UNIT 4

[1] M.M. Wolf, D.K. Giles, and R.V. Hall, "Experiments with Token Reinforcement in a Remedial Classroom," *Behaviour Research and Therapy*, VI (1968), 51-64.

[2] K.D. O'Leary and W.C. Becker, "Behavior Modification of an Adjustment Class: A Token Reinforcement Program," *Exceptional Children*, XXXIII (1967), 637-642.

Unit 4 • Exercise 1

1. Some children don't care. They are turned———————
   by people and their world.

2. This can happen when much of a day involves one
   ————————————— experience after another.

3. Large changes can be made in these children by switching
   from the use of ————————————— and punishment to
   the use of praise and other —————————————.

4. Teresa seemed ————————————— upset to her mother.
   She was unhappy at home and school.

5. When a ————————————— system was established at
   home and school, Teresa became a happy girl again.

6. The reward system involved giving Teresa —————————
   each day for various tasks at home and —————————.

7. Teresa's teacher would send home a —————————————
   each day indicating how many —————————————
   Teresa had earned and how she had earned them.

8. Teresa received ————————————— on Saturday according to the number of points she earned that week.

9. Teresa earned ————————————— points the first week
   and ————————————— points the second week.

10. Teresa's mother decided it was really worthwhile to focus
    on the ————————————— and to use rewards instead
    of punishments.

11. Many children have been taught that school work leads to _____ and punishment.

12. They skip school and often _____ _____ of school.

13. When children have learned that school work usually results in failure it may be necessary to use strong, obvious, and _____ reinforcers for each appropriate response.

14. In addition to stronger reinforcers it is desirable to use teaching programs which permit _____.

15. Token reinforcement systems are one practical way to introduce _____ reinforcers into the classroom or the home.

16. There are four rules to be observed in the design of a token system. We know that immediate reinforcers are more effective than delayed reinforcers; therefore, start with tokens which can be quickly and _____ given.

17. A variety of payoffs increases the chances that you will have a _____ for most children.

18. Token reinforcers serve as _____ reinforcers which can be traded for many effective reinforcers.

19. In designing a token system, we should reinforce a _____ early in the program, and gradually reinforce _____ as the behavior improves.

20. To make it possible to get off the system, tokens should be _____ with praise and affection so that these social reinforcers will gain reinforcing power.

21. Presentation of tokens should be paired with other events which we wish to gain ———————————— properties.

22. Saying "good job" just before or as you hand a child a token will eventually result in "good job" gaining the same ———————————— power as the token.

23. The tokens in the Wolf, Giles, and Hall study were ———————————— on a card.

24. The check marks satisfy the first rule in designing token systems which requires that tokens be ————————————— and ———————————— given.

25. The cards full of points could be traded in for a variety of goods and events such as a circus, zoo, etc. The ———————————— of events which could be earned by the tokens satisfies the second rule in designing token systems.

26. When a child first joined the program he earned a point for each problem, but later the amount and difficulty of the work required to earn points was ————————————. This is an example of the third rule concerning the use of a lot of reinforcement in the beginning and ———————————— as the behavior improves.

27. O'Leary and Becker devised a ———————————— system which was used by one teacher in a class of seventeen problem children.

28. Step-by-step the teacher increased the length of time that went by before the tokens could be ———————————— in for the reinforcers.

29. Points could be traded for a _____ of reinforcers such as candy, comics, perfume and kites.

30. Presentation of points and trading in of points for prizes was paired with _____ from the teacher.

31. Jimmy was aggressive and did not complete classroom assignments. Tokens for Jimmy consisted of _____ which he took home to his mother. The notes earned time in which Jimmy could _____ _____.

32. Aaron did not work in class. He messed around and played with his friends. In addition he _____ other children on the way to and from school. Tokens for Aaron consisted of _____ _____ on the board.

33. Aaron earned one check mark for each _____ minutes of good working behavior.

34. Aaron could exchange ten check marks for thirty minutes of time in which he supervised younger children in the use of _____ _____. Since the young children could not use the tools unless Aaron was there, they liked him to come.

35. Aaron learned to work in the classroom and to work _____ with younger children.

36. Mrs. James gave out _____ to her four boys when they were being cooperative.

37. She tried to give out from _____ to _____ tickets to each boy each day.

38. When she gave the tickets, she _____ the boys and told them what she saw them doing that she liked.

39. The first week the tickets could be traded for a movie and _____ _____.

40. Mrs. James reported that giving tickets helped her to remember to _____ her boys for cooperating, instead of always _____ them after they got into a fight.

41. Lynn earned _____ on a chart to help her stop thumbsucking.

42. With children, bribery usually refers to the situation where the child _____ _____ do something, and the parent "ups the ante" to try to get the child to behave.

43. This is not a good procedure because the child gets rewarded for _____ _____ what he is supposed to do.

44. The proper use of rewards will teach children to learn to do what we want them to _____.

45. The general rule to be learned from the examples in the unit is that if the usual methods of reinforcing behavior do not work, then the parent should _____ his procedures to find _____ reinforcers.

Check your answers in the back of the book. Where you have made errors, study the unit again.

Unit 4 • Exercise 2

A BEHAVIOR CHANGE PROJECT

Devise a token reinforcement system to change the target behavior from Unit 3, Exercise 2.

1. Describe your target behavior.

   _____

   _____

2. If this is a behavior to be weakened, describe the incompatible behavior to be reinforced:

   _____

   _____

3. Describe the token reinforcement system for your target behavior, or for the incompatible behavior if you are trying to weaken the target behavior.
   a. What is the token reinforcer?

      _____

      _____

   b. How is it given?

      _____

      _____

   c. What is the payoff?

      _____

      _____

   d. Is praise given? Describe:

      _____

      _____

4. If you are using a point chart or a star chart, draw a copy of your chart on a separate page and fill in the daily points earned by your child.

5. Record each day, using the chart on the next page, an estimate of how often the target behavior occurs and any comments you have about it.

TARGET BEHAVIOR _____

DAY	HOW OFTEN DID IT OCCUR TODAY?	COMMENTS
1.		
2.		
3.		
4.		
5.		
6.		
7.		
8.		
9.		
10.		
11.		
12.		
13.		
14.		

Unit 5

REINFORCEMENT AND PUNISHMENT IN EVERYDAY LIFE

The adventures of Gwendolyn

Gwen is racing through the woods, frightened, almost terrified. Some strange man or creature is chasing her. She dares not look back long enough to make sure. As she hurries between trees and bushes, she notices she is running with her hands over her ears. She starts to take her hands down from her ears so she can run better, but puts them right back. The noise from the beast is unbearable. As she comes over a small rise, the ground seems to open up in front of her and she is falling, falling, falling . . . the noise is getting louder and louder again. With a frightened startle, she wakes up. She looks at the beastly alarm clock for a moment, and then turns it off.

Another day starts.

The behavior of waking and turning off an alarm clock is reinforced by the stopping of the irritating alarm. In everyday life, our moment to moment behaviors are controlled by reinforcing and punishing events. Let's follow Gwendolyn for a while and notice some of the events in her life which are consequent events for moment to moment behavior. Our objective is to develop in you skills in self-observation, so that you can more readily see events which influence your behaviors as examples of reinforcing and punishing events. Try to identify important consequences as you read. Later the exercises will also help you to pin them down.

Still groggy, Gwen sits up on the side of her bed. The floor is freezing. She quickly reaches for her bathrobe lying across the foot of her bed, tucks her toes into her slippers and tries to make her way to the bathroom. She stumbles into the door frame. It is punishing her clumsy behavior. She goes down the hall, making it safely through the next door frame.

She glances in the mirror as she moves to prepare a shower, glad that Reggie doesn't see her like this, thinking he would never agree to marry her if he did. The water is freezing. Gwen jumps back from the shower, reaching at the same time to turn it off. She is being punished again for not paying close attention to what is going on. Shivering and half blue, she starts again, running the water until it gets warm, making sure it doesn't get too warm, and flips up the shower control once again. That is more like it. A warmth engulfs her as she bathes and plans her day. She stands there for a long time and soaks up the warmth and comforting patter of the water against her flesh.

As she dries her hair, she begins to think about breakfast. She is starving. At 116 pounds, she doesn't need to worry about her weight, yet she does. Her mother is overweight and Gwen vows to herself that she is always going to be more sensible about food.

On her way to the kitchen, she stops to wake Jimmy. She sits on the edge of his bed and shakes him gently. He wakes slowly, but when he sees his mother, he smiles. Gwen smiles back and gives him a hug.

GWEN: Time to get up, Jimmy. What would you like for breakfast?

JIMMY: Sugar Pops, Mom.

GWEN: Okay, get washed and dressed and I'll have it ready for you.

Gwen has only thirty minutes for breakfast and getting Jimmy ready to drop off at her mother's. She quickly fixes some instant coffee, a poached egg, and toast for herself. She eats nearly the same thing every morning, and never seems to tire of it.

Jimmy appears dressed except for his shirt, shoes, and socks. He sits down on the chair by the kitchen table and pushes his feet out for help.

Gwen quickly slips on his socks and shoes and ties his laces without saying anything. She wonders when he will learn to tie his own shoes. She doesn't seem to find time to teach him in the morning. They are always so rushed, and it never seems important in the evening.

Before he eats, she sends him to put on his plaid shirt. Jimmy, without a word, goes back to get the shirt.

They finish breakfast quickly and quietly and head for the car. Gwen helps Jimmy with the zipper on his coat and holds his hand as they walk to the car in the drive. It is a beautiful morning for March. It is still cold. The ground is lightly covered with snow, but the street is clear. The sun is bright and it is going to get warmer. The air smells clean and fresh compared to the closed-up apartment.

Gwen helps Jimmy into the car and gets out the scraper to clear the windows. As she gets in and is about to put the key in the ignition, she panics, afraid it won't start and forcing her to be late again because she has been putting off getting a new battery. She is afraid to turn the key. She pumps the gas pedal once to set the choke, depresses the gas pedal a little, and turns the key to start position. The starting motor growls and the engine turns slowly through the thick oil. She stops, waits a moment, and tries again. This time the engine turns over faster and catches. Gwen heaves a sigh of relief, smiles to herself, and backs out of the garage ready to conquer the world. Her 1954 Ford started again! She usually has confidence in her "old" car, but the failure of a week ago is still fresh in her mind.

It is two blocks to her mother's. Gwen doesn't stop in, but just lets Jimmy off when her mother responds to her toot. She and Jimmy give each other a hug and a kiss.

Jimmy is quite a big boy for a six year old. He stays with his grandmother until it is time to walk to school, and then returns there after school. Gwen thinks he is doing pretty well without a father; in fact, she is quite proud of him. She wishes she had more time for him. She worries about the fact that he is so quiet.

The trip to the office on Lincoln Avenue is uneventful. As she passes Elmwood, Gwen sees the flashing red light of a police car who has stopped a young man apparently for speeding. She recalls the last time she got a ticket, doing forty in a thirty mile zone. This is a good place for a radar speed trap. It cost her fifteen dollars. She sympathizes with the driver getting the ticket, but also checks her speed. She can use fifteen dollars better than giving it to the city. Besides, she can't afford to lose her driver's license. There just aren't any buses that can get her to work.

Interstate Insurance is a relatively new company serving mainly midwestern states. Gwen is secretary to Mr. R. Donald Bear. Some days she believes he is a bear, but usually he is a happy, though blunt, boss. She likes working for him and affectionately talks about him as "our Bear" instead of R. Bear. He usually doesn't come to the office before noon, since he often works in the evenings, but there is a stack of work ready for Gwen. She fixes a cup of coffee, takes a sip, then settles into typing letters, forms, estimates, and proposals.

MARGE: [*Arriving*] Good morning, Gwen. [*Marge is twenty-five, single, quite attractive and proud of being independent.*]

GWEN: Hi, Marge. Good to see you. [*Gwen and Marge have worked together for only four months, but Gwen considers Marge her closest friend.*]

MARGE: Did you see Reggie last night?

GWEN: [*Hesitates, wondering why Marge is asking her about Reggie*] Yes.

MARGE: What did he say about Saturday?

GWEN: [*Remembering their plans to double date Saturday night*] Oh! He said fine to bowling and then pizza at your place.

MARGE: Good. Tom can go too.

GWEN: [*Taken back a little by this, but not wanting Marge to see it*] I need to get some work out before R. Bear shows. See you at coffee break. [*Gwen turns to the letter in her typewriter.*] [*To herself*] Tom is coming. [*Her thoughts drift back to last summer at the beach. In many ways Tom really turns her on. But most of the time he treats her like one of the boys. He is too casual with Gwen to really please her, and besides she can't go out with him if he doesn't ask her. She is still wondering why she introduced Tom and Marge to each other.*]

Gwen gets back to work. If she doesn't please R. Bear she will be without a paycheck.

MARGE: [*Stopping on the way to the lounge*] Break time, Gwen.

GWEN: Those two hours went fast. I barely made a dent in R. Bear's correspondence. You know, I really don't feel comfortable until that "in" box is empty, and I'm caught up. But it rarely seems to happen. There's always a little more to do.

MARGE: [*They start for the lounge.*] You're too compulsive, Gwen. In some ways, you try to please your boss too much. Have you thought about turning it around now and then?

GWEN: What do you mean?

MARGE: Set it up so he has to try to please you now and then.

GWEN: [*Puzzled*] I still don't get it.

MARGE: How long have you been here?

GWEN: Since June, about ten months.

MARGE: Have you asked for a raise yet?

GWEN: No.

MARGE: Have you worked over time?

GWEN: Yes, almost every week.

MARGE: Have you talked about taking another job?

GWEN: No.

MARGE: See what I mean? You do everything to please R. Bear, but he hasn't gone out of his way for you, except to smile now and then. [*Marge hands Gwen a cup of coffee and they sit by the corner table. They are alone.*]

GWEN: Marge, you know I'm not that kind of person . . . I don't go around *setting things up*. I'm just me.

MARGE: Gwen, I'm just talking about using the bargaining power you have. The business world clearly runs on a bargaining basis, but *you* don't bargain. You give your bargaining power away. Free. When you know you are doing a good job, you shouldn't be afraid to ask for favors or a raise. I am not supposed to talk about it, but I got a fifteen dollar a month raise at the end of my ninety-day time period. I just talked to my boss about it. He agreed I was worth it and made the recommendation to Jordan.

GWEN: I can sort of see what you mean. Maybe if I find the right time, I'll ask. [*To herself*] You know I was the same way with Tom, as I am now with Reggie. I try too hard to please and they just take advantage of me. Why don't people appreciate what they have? . . . [*Gwen pursues the question with Marge.*] Marge, did you ever notice that men seem to want what they don't have, more than what they do have?

MARGE: You mean the grass is always greener on the other side?

GWEN: Sort of.

MARGE: Why restrict it to men? Women act the same way sometimes.

GWEN: You have a point there. But men seem more that way to me. Anyway, I'd like to figure out what that's about. [*Gwen wonders if Marge knows how she feels about Tom.*]

MARGE: Do you want me to help you?

GWEN: I think so. You seem to see these things a little more clearly than I do . . . and you are right about my not bargaining with my boss.

MARGE: Okay. How long have you been dating Reggie?

GWEN: Since September.

MARGE: Have you dated anyone else?

GWEN: No.

MARGE: Have you threatened to leave him when he has dated other girls?

GWEN: No. But I have no special claim to him. We aren't engaged. And he is good to Jimmy.

MARGE: Does he make demands of you?

GWEN: Sure. We go to the places he likes. They're usually too noisy for me. But he likes them. We go out when he asks me, not necessarily when I'm lonely. He doesn't show up sometimes. He can get pretty rude if he drinks, but I'm not supposed to get angry with him. Is that what you mean by demands?

MARGE: Exactly, Gwen! And do you make demands of him?

GWEN: Very few. If I'm unhappy, I just keep quiet awhile. I usually just try to please him. Isn't that what loving is about?

MARGE: Are you happy with him?

GWEN: Not really. That's why I wanted to talk about it.

MARGE: Does he like you?

GWEN: He says he does. He keeps asking me out and sort of assumes we go together.

MARGE: Just like R. Bear. Gwen, can't you see the parallel? You give Reggie what he wants from you, but you are not *training him* to please you in return, except on his special terms. You give away your bargaining power, free. Did it ever occur to you that we sort of train other people to be nice to us by the way in which we are nice to them? You work hard to please R. Bear,

71

whether or not he asks you to work after hours, whether or not he lets you off early when you ask. By asking nothing in return, you train R. Bear to treat you any way he feels at the moment. You don't seem to complain. But I think he gets pretty inconsiderate with you and you've taught him to be that way.

GWEN: Marge, that's going too far, R. Bear is very considerate as far as I'm concerned . . . What do you mean *train Reggie to please me?*

MARGE: It's a give and take sort of thing. You suggest to him something you would like to do with him. After all, he really doesn't know unless you tell him. If he follows your suggestion, you show him with words and affection how pleased you are with his thoughtfulness. You then work to learn to like something that really pleases him.

GWEN: You really do mean train, don't you? I've never thought about people that way, except maybe Jimmy. [*Gwen puts down her coffee cup and they both stand facing each other.*]

MARGE: And Gwen, if he consistently displeases you, you may have to let him know this, too.

GWEN: Do you think I should date someone else to make him jealous?

MARGE: Not to make him jealous. But you should date other fellas, just so you won't be so dependent on Reggie. It puts you in a more equal bargaining position with him. He's going to want to learn to do more to please you if he's not so sure you'll be there any time he wants you. If he wants to be with you, he has to keep working at pleasing you, because it is possible that someone else will please you more.

GWEN: [*They head back to their desks.*] I'm going to have to think about this awhile. Have lunch with me?

MARGE: Okay.

Gwen keeps running through the ideas Marge had triggered. The grass is greener on the other side . . . men want what they don't have . . . No. That's not it at all. According to what Marge said, we do what we teach each other to do. I teach Reggie to be inconsiderate of me and to go out with girls by the way I respond to him. What a strange idea. I wonder how I do it, if I really do?

During the next hour Gwen works away at letters and estimates, takes a few messages for R. Bear, and continues to ruminate about her discussion with Marge. She begins to think maybe Marge was right about some of it, and maybe she can test it out a bit with R. Bear.

R. Bear comes swinging in at 11:30. He gives Gwen a brief "hi" as she lifts his messages and mail for him to grab on the way by to the inner office. Gwen gets up and brings him his cup of coffee.

GWEN: Is there anything else you need?

R. BEAR: Not right now, but I want to talk to you later about putting in some extra time. We're getting behind again.

GWEN: [*A little hesitant*] Can I ask you a question?

R. BEAR: Sure, fire.

GWEN: Do you really like my work? Do you think I do a good job?

R. BEAR: Of course. Don't I tell you that twice a week? You're the best secretary I've ever had. What's the matter?

GWEN: [*Looking down a little frightened*] Well, if I am so good and work hard for you, why is it that some people who have been working in the office less than I earn more?

R. Bear is surprised at the question. Gwen had never spoken of money before. He was planning a raise for June. His boss Jordan would probably approve it earlier if he asked him to.

R. BEAR: Do you think you deserve more money?

GWEN: Yes.

R. BEAR: How about ten dollars more the first of the month?

GWEN: How about twenty dollars? [*She couldn't believe she said it.*]

R. BEAR: I think we can arrange that. Give me time to see Jordan and I'll let you know later. [*Gwen practically skips out of R. Bear's office and gets ready to meet Marge for lunch.*]

Gwen doesn't say anything about it until they are seated in the booth. She is ready to burst, holding her new success in until they are away from the rest of the office staff and by themselves.

GWEN: Guess what? I asked for a raise! I asked for a raise!

MARGE: Did you get it?

GWEN: I think so. He suggested ten dollars. I said, "How about twenty dollars?" And he said he would check it with Jordan, but he thought it was o.k. That's $240 a year more.

MARGE: That's great. But I thought you didn't care about money.

GWEN: Jimmy and I might find some way to use it. [*Pause*] Let me buy your lunch to celebrate and sort of say thanks for your help.

MARGE: Sure, I'd like that too. [*Their sandwiches come and they begin to eat lunch quietly.*]

GWEN: Marge, I was thinking about some of the things that happened to me this morning getting up. The floor was cold so I quickly reached for my bathrobe and slippers. I bumped into a doorway and got hurt, so I looked more carefully at the next doorway. Then I got frozen in a cold shower and had to turn it off and warm it up before starting again. You know, I've never paid attention to things like that before, but the series of incidents keeps saying to me "your surroundings control you." I'm not sure I like that.

MARGE: It's a good thing you're not a Polar Eskimo.

GWEN: How's that?

MARGE: Can you imagine living in an environment where the average winter temperature is minus forty degrees? That exerts a considerable control over you.

GWEN: How do you know so much? You seem to be the well-spring of knowledge today.

MARGE: I've been reading a paperback about the Polar Eskimos. Almost everything they do is guided by the battle to survive starvation and coldness. They have little privacy 'cause it is impractical to heat a house more than fifteen feet in diameter. It's too cold to bathe. It's sometimes necessary to kill dogs they need and love, if hunting is poor and there is nothing to eat. Often families are isolated from each other for months at a time while searching for food.

GWEN: I wouldn't like that at all. When you look at it that way, we really have a friendly environment, even at thirty-one degrees on a March morning.

MARGE: Gwen, you said that you didn't like the idea of your surroundings controlling you. But you know they do, whether you like it or not, just as they do for the Eskimos, sailors, desert Arabs, or jungle dwellers.

GWEN: [Agreeing] You're right. But isn't it funny that we usually don't think it controls us?

MARGE: That's usually because we have *learned* to live with our environment. It has taught us how to survive in it with a minimum of punishment. It's only when we get hurt by it that we really pay attention. Just look at all the things people do to avoid being hurt by their environment. We make buildings, beds, air conditioners, food storage facilities, heaters, and so on. You might say that nowadays we build the environment that controls us.

GWEN: [*She really liked that idea.*] We build the environment that controls us . . . We do it in ways that make us happier. I don't think I mind being controlled by an environment that I can help control. That doesn't sound so bad.

MARGE: You're silly, Gwen. It makes no difference whether you mind or not. That's the way it is.

GWEN: Marge, when we left our coffee break this morning, you said something about how we make each other what we are by the way we react to each other. Like I teach Reggie to be inconsiderate and my boss to take advantage of me. Is that really true?

MARGE: Gwen, you just agreed with the idea when you said "we build the environment that controls us."

GWEN: [*Still puzzled*] Well, that's different, isn't it?

MARGE: The principle is the same. We do what we are taught to do, whether by other people or by the physical environment. We do more of the things that are nice or fun, and do less of the things that hurt us. That's all. If we can provide the right kind of consequences for each other's behavior, we ought to be able to make each other happier people. [*Her thoughts flash back to Kansas University and the long discussions she had with her psychology instructor about changing people.*]

GWEN: I think it would be fun to try to build a world with happier people. Hey, we better get back to work. It's almost one o'clock. [*Crossing the street*] Well, I did one thing about the environment that controls me today.

MARGE: What's that?

GWEN: I got it to give me a twenty dollar raise. [*They both laugh and go inside.*]

R. BEAR: [*Buzzing Gwen*] Jordan okayed your raise. You deserve it. Thought you would like to know. Sit down.

GWEN: Thank you. That is good news. [*She smiles at him.*]

R. BEAR: I have some letters to dictate to you. [*Gwen already has pad and pencil ready.*] But before we start, let's get the over-time settled. How about tonight?

GWEN: [*While he is talking, she notices that he looks at her legs almost as much as her eyes. She doesn't mind.*] Oh! I have a date. I could work tomorrow evening though.

R. BEAR: Okay. Just be sure these proposals are in the mail by Friday morning. [*He hands Gwen more than a dozen insurance coverage proposals he drafted out the night before. He takes out a cigarette and leans back in his chair as he is dictating, staring at the ceiling.*]

Gwen wonders why he continues to smoke with all the evidence on cancer . . .

The dictation goes on until 3:20. She almost misses Marge at the lounge, but they have ten minutes together.

Gwen wants to talk more with Marge about Saturday. She is a little afraid of being so close to Tom Saturday night, and she knows she is not going to change Reggie overnight, even with Marge's help.

GWEN: Marge, I've been thinking about what you said about training Reggie, and making my bargaining power more equal, and doing more to control "the environment that controls me" . . . I like that phrase. You know, I like my raise too . . . Anyway, [*slowly pacing each word*] how would . . . you . . . feel . . . if . . . I . . . dated Tom . . . now and then . . . [*Afraid, hesitating*] if I could get him to "invite" me out.

MARGE: [*Never expecting this from Gwen, looks hurt for a moment. Then she catches herself.*] Gwen, you know Tom and I are just good friends and we both date others. It might confuse *our* relationship a little, but it might be fun, too.

GWEN: [*Throwing her arms around Marge*] You are great! [*They hug for a moment.*] I thought I never could bring myself to talk about Tom with you. Thanks for not getting up tight.

MARGE: Do you like Tom?

GWEN: I have for a long time. We went out together just for a short time last year and then he didn't ask me out anymore.

MARGE: Gwen, I have an idea . . . if we work together as a team, maybe we can shape these lunk heads up . . . what do you say? . . .

GWEN: [*Excited*] Okay . . . but how do we do it?

[*Later*]

Before leaving work, Gwen calls Reggie and cancels her date for the evening without explanation, but confirms bowling on Saturday. Gwen thinks Reggie seems disappointed. She decides this is a good sign.

Gwen picks up Jimmy. They have a light supper, clean up and watch TV for awhile. When the first commercial comes on, Gwen goes to the refrigerator for a Coke and pours some in a cup for Jimmy. When she returns, the commercial is still running full blast, twice as loud as the rest of the show. She remembers reading about the TV ratings put out by the water company in a big city. By watching the water flow meters they could judge which shows were more popular. The water flow rates would go up very high at commercial times. She laughs to herself thinking about the guys at the water company watching the meters and several TV sets and writing it all down. Gwen thinks the ad agencies must be missing the boat, if everyone leaves when the commercials come on. Now, she wishes she had a remote control to turn off that loud commercial.

Jimmy plays on the floor with some trucks while half watching the TV. He doesn't care much for the shows Mommy watches, but he likes being near her.

At 7:30 Gwen fixes Jimmy's bath and stays with him while he gets ready for bed. She reads a chapter from his library book on space travel before saying good night.

Gwen is uneasy and anxious. She doesn't know why. She wants Jimmy to get to sleep so she can be alone for awhile.

[*A little before nine, the phone rings*]

TOM: Hey! How about if I bring over a six-pack and we talk a little?

GWEN: I'd like that, Tom.

TOM: Okay, see you in a few minutes.

GWEN: [*Surprised*] Why, all of a sudden, did Tom call? I wonder what Marge is up to.

While waiting Gwen thinks back to what Marge had said about her giving away her bargaining power, and how we teach people to be nice to us. Now she has a real chance to test it with Tom.

ANNOUNCER:
Tune in next week for the continuing, exciting, true to life . . . Adventures of Gwendolyn. Will Gwendolyn get Tom or Reggie? Why did Tom come then? What will happen Saturday evening? Is it possible that Marge is really interested in *Reggie?*

[*Fade*]

Unit 5 • Exercise 1

Place one word in each blank. Return to the unit as needed.

1. Behaviors which reduce or eliminate unpleasant events are
    _____ by such events. For example, turn-
    ing off an alarm, or jumping back from a cold shower.

2. When Gwendolyn stumbled into the door frame on her way
    to the bathroom, she was _____ for her
    clumsy behavior and for not attending to what she was
    doing.

3. The shower also _____ her for not paying
    close _____ to what she was doing by
    spraying her with cold water.

4. Careful adjustment of the shower controls was
    _____ by the reinforcing feeling of the
    warm and comforting shower waters.

5. When Jimmy smiled, his mother smiled back and gave him
    a hug. Jimmy's smile was _____ by his
    mother.

6. When Gwen asked Jimmy what he would like for breakfast,
    she was pointing out a desirable _____
    waiting for Jimmy as soon as he got dressed. This procedure
    would likely lead to Jimmy's getting dressed _____
    than just telling Jimmy to get dressed.

7. Even the same old breakfast can taste good and be
    _____ if we haven't eaten for a while.

8. When Mommy put on Jimmy's shoes and socks, she reinforced Jimmy's _____ _____ _____.

9. Gwendolyn had been punished by her car's failure to start, but today she was _____ by the car starting.

10. On the way to work Gwendolyn checked her speed when she saw the flashing red light of a police car. She had previously been _____ for speeding by getting a ticket. The flashing red light now functions as a learned _____ for speeding.

11. Marge and Gwen talked during their break about "bargaining power." Bargaining power can be translated into the behavioral concept of making reinforcers

_____ (on a desired behavior).

12. When you "give away" your _____

_____, you have dispensed your reinforcers non-contingently.

13. Marge told Gwen that she had trained R. Bear to be

_____ of her by working hard to please him whether or not he asked her to work overtime, failed to give pay raises, etc.

14. The key to Marge's philosophy lies in the sentence that says, "We sort of have to train other people to be nice to us by the _____ in which we are nice to them."

15. At lunch Gwen presented the conclusion that "Your surroundings _____ you." Marge replied with the example about the Polar Eskimos.

16. We change our behaviors to survive in a given environment with a minimum of _____.

17. Men make buildings, beds, air conditioners, food storage facilities, heaters, etc. in order to avoid being hurt by their _____.

18. In many ways, we build the environment that _____ us.

19. When we are working on building our physical environment, we almost always attempt to change it in ways that will make us _____.

20. The same principle can apply to our social _____. Other people control many of the things we do. However, if the things we do don't make us happy, then we can try to change our social environment by _____ other people different ways to respond to us.

21. One might guess that a lot of people keep smoking because the immediate reinforcing effects of smoking are stronger than the anticipated future _____ associated with cancer.

22. One might say that friends have learned to _____ each other.

23. A lot of TV commercials do not _____ attending to them.

24. Reading to Jimmy can serve to reward his getting _____ _____ _____.

25. My guess is that Gwendolyn will get _____.

Unit 5 • Exercise 2

List the consequences of the behaviors listed.

BEHAVIOR   CONSEQUENCE

1. turned off alarm clock   1. _____

2. sat up with feet on floor   2. _____

3. bumped into door frame   3. _____

4. walked through door   4. _____

5. glanced in mirror   5. _____

6. turned on shower   6. _____

7. turned off shower   7. _____

8. adjusted water temperature 8. _____

9. stood in shower   9. _____

10. fixed breakfast   10. _____

11. Jimmy said, "Help me,
    Mommy."   11. _____

12. turned key to start the
    second time   12. _____

13. "Goodbye, Mommy."   13. _____

14. saw a police car and
    checked speed   14. _____

15. fixed a cup of coffee   15. _____

16. "Did you see Reggie last
    night?"   16. _____

17. Working to please R. Bear   17. _____

18. asking for a raise   18. _____

19. Gwen threw her arms
    around Marge   19. _____

20. picking up the telephone
    when Tom called   20. _____

Check your answers with those in the back of the book. Where you have made errors, study the unit again.

Be sure to continue your token project, Unit 4, Exercise 2, pages 62-64.

Unit 6

WHY PARENTS AND TEACHERS GOOF:
THE CRITICISM TRAP

The more teachers say "sit down" the more they stand up

It was 9:20 a.m. in a first grade of forty-eight children taught by two teachers. Two rooms were available for the class with a movable wall between them. The children's desks were grouped into six tables of eight children each. They have been assigned work to do at their seats, while the two young and capable teachers teach reading in small groups.

Two observers* entered the room, sat down, and for the next twenty minutes they recorded the number of children out of their seats during each ten-second period. Observations were made for six days. The observers also recorded how often the teachers told the children to sit down, or to get back in their seats.

During these first six days about three children were out of their seats every ten seconds. The teachers would say "sit down" about seven times in a twenty-minute period.

Then, some very strange events began to occur. The teachers were asked to tell the children to "sit down" more often. During the next twelve days the teachers said "sit down" 27.5 times each twenty minutes. *The children stood up more*—an average of 4.5 children standing every ten seconds.

We tried it again. For the next eight days, the teachers went back to saying "sit down" only seven times in twenty minutes. Out of seat behavior declined to an average of three times per ten seconds.

---

observers: College students trained to record teacher and child behavior.

Again, we asked the teachers to tell the children to "sit down" more often (twenty-eight times in twenty minutes). *The children stood up more again*—four times every ten seconds.

Finally, we asked the teachers to quit telling the children to sit down, but rather to praise sitting and working. They did this well, and less than two children were standing every ten seconds, the lowest standing observed.[1]

What can be going on? How do we explain such happenings? There is one additional puzzling fact. The children *actually did sit down when asked by the teacher to do so,* so the result wasn't due to a few children standing up a lot.

CONSIDER THE FOLLOWING:

Child stands up **Teacher says "sit down"** **Child sits down**

The teacher's saying "sit down" *follows* standing up. When the teacher says "sit down" more often, the children stand up more often. When the teacher says "sit down" less often, the children stand up less often. "Sit down" is a reinforcing consequence for standing up. "Sit down" is an event following a response which strengthens that response. It *is* a reinforcer for standing up.

But "sit down" also has another effect on the response of sitting. The children do sit down when told to, so "sit down" must *also* be a signal for sitting.

What a beautiful trap! Imagine, the teacher thinks that telling the children to "sit down" works, because they *do sit down.* But that is only the immediate effect. The effect on standing is not seen until later and might be missed unless you learn what to look for. The teacher's words are having exactly the opposite effect on standing from that which she desires.

Making a "bad" class out of a good one

In one study we took a "good" class and made it into a "bad" one for a few weeks by having the teacher no longer praise the children. When the teacher no longer praised the children, off-task behavior increased from 8.7 per cent to 25.5 per cent. The teacher criticized off-task behaviors and did not praise on-task behaviors.

When we asked the teacher to increase her criticism from five times in twenty minutes to sixteen times in twenty minutes, the children showed even more off-task behavior. Off-task behavior increased to an average of 31.2 per cent and on some days was above fifty per cent. *Attention to the off-task behavior increased it.* A return to praising brought back good working behavior.[2]

Parents get caught too

Imagine the situation of the parent who tries to teach her child mainly by scolding rather than praising. A child misbehaves, she catches him and scolds him, and he stops for now. *Scolding and criticizing seems to work. The parent is reinforced for scolding, by the child stopping his misbehavior for awhile.* She is trapped by being reinforced for scolding. The very same behaviors she does not want may be increased. It will then be necessary to scold more. It is a trap. Only by clearly seeing what is going on can the parent avoid this trap and behave in ways which will help her child best.

Peter's mother was caught by the criticism trap

In Unit 1 we told about a four-year-old boy, Peter, who was very demanding and difficult to control. His mother did not know what to do next to better the situation. The clear use of reinforcement for good behaviors and punishment of objectionable behaviors produced a quick change in Peter (and his mother).

Peter got most of his attention from his mother by misbehaving. If Peter did behave, Mother probably took that time to get some of her chores done and to care for her other three children. Very likely Peter's mother taught Peter to misbehave.

She was caught in the criticism trap. Over time from birth, Peter got more and more attention from his mother for bad behavior, and *less and less* attention for good behavior. The more Mother criticized, scolded, and tried to punish, the worse Peter got. Only when she clearly rewarded Peter for good behavior did he get better.

 Criticism does not always work this way. If a parent is using reward and praise for good behaviors, then a little criticism will not hurt. It is only when the MAIN WAY in which a child gets attention from adults is through criticism that we run into the criticism trap.

A RELATED TRAP—GIVING IN

 Just as criticism is usually not an effective punishment, other forms of punishment can be made ineffective if used the wrong way. A common fault parents get trapped into is to rightly punish, perhaps a little too severely, and then feel sorry for the child and let him have his way, anyway. This teaches your child that misbehavior pays off and that punishment is followed by rewards. It may even teach your child to misbehave to get you to punish him so that then you will be nice to him.

How to escape the criticism trap

To escape the criticism trap, it is necessary for the parent to make it possible to praise more and criticize less. This can be done by:
1. Providing for cues or reminders to praise more.
2. Getting practice in how to praise.
3. Making it possible to be reinforced for praising more. (Usually the improvement in your child is the best reinforcer, but that may take a little time.)

PROVIDING FOR CUES OR REMINDERS TO PRAISE MORE

Give out tokens to prompt your praising. Imagine a situation where a parent has to give out an average of fifteen tokens each day to four children. Now also imagine that the parent is instructed to tell her children what they did well or improved on to earn the tokens. The stage is set for the parent to be praising at least sixty times each day. The tokens can be used to cue praising. The effect on a parent's behavior can be amazing.

To use this procedure to learn to praise more, the parent needs only a supply of "things" she can pass out and some pay-off when they are turned back in. Actually, one could also use food like raisins, or jelly beans as the "things" passed out. Remember to praise when you give out the tokens or treats.

Put up signs to remind you to praise. Notes stuck on the refrigerator, the kitchen cabinets, the back of the bathroom door, or your dressing table can serve as cues to remind you what you are about. The signs might look like these:

ASK ABOUT SCHOOL

When you praise, DESCRIBE what Jim did WELL

DON'T WAIT for misbehavior

PRAISE

REWARD IMPROVEMENT

Tell Joe what he did RIGHT

Catch them being GOOD

PRAISE MARY

GETTING PRACTICE IN HOW TO PRAISE

Some parents need help in learning how to be good praisers. In the next unit, exercises are provided to give practice in praising and in using other reinforcers. The key is to think about all the situations where you now criticize a lot, and figure out what would be the positive way to deal with those situations.

For example, Jimmy comes running into the house for dinner and throws his coat on the floor and leaves the door open. What can you do besides shouting at him?

You might say: "Jimmy, we would be glad to have you join us for dinner after you close the door and hang up your coat." Then thank him when he does those things.

At dinner, Bill and Glenda try to talk to you while you are having a talk with Father. What do you do?

You might finish your talk, ignoring the talking out of turn. When you are through, say to your husband, "Did you see how polite Mark was when we were talking? He just listened and didn't interrupt." Mark is the third child. He did not talk out. He can be used as an example to the others as to what are good manners. Later when Bill and Glenda give examples of not interrupting, praise them too.

These examples are provided here just to give you an idea about what we mean when we talk about practicing how to praise. The actual practice goes with the next unit.

GETTING REINFORCEMENT FOR PRAISING MORE
Usually when we start being more positive with others, they get more positive with us. When you praise your children more, they are likely to do things which please you more.

It is also possible to ask those around you (husband, older children) to say nice things to you for praising more.

However, it sometimes takes a "little doing" to get things started. As an exercise for the coming week, we have suggested that you record how often you praise and criticize during dinner for the coming week. Then next week we will see if you can change that. The exercise sets up a method to help you keep a daily check on your progress. Actually, seeing that a desired change is taking place is a good reinforcer for most adults.

Summary

The criticism trap consists of thinking criticism works because the criticized behavior stops for a bit, when in fact the criticized behavior is being reinforced.

This is most likely to happen when most of the attention received from adults is in the form of criticism and punishment.
   You can escape the criticism trap by:
1.   Providing for cues or reminders to praise more.
2.   Getting practice in how to praise.
3.   Making it possible to be reinforced for praising more.

While we have emphasized increasing praise behavior as a way out of the criticism trap, actually we are talking about increasing the use of reinforcers generally and reducing the use of criticism and punishment.

The next unit deals with how to reinforce.

NOTES TO UNIT 6

[1] C.H. Madsen, Jr., W.C. Becker, D.R. Thomas, Linda Koser, and Elaine Plager, "An Analysis of the Reinforcing Function of 'Sit Down' Commands," *Readings in Educational Psychology*, ed. R.K. Parker (Boston: Allyn and Bacon, 1968).

[2] D.R. Thomas, W.C. Becker, and Marianne Armstrong, "Production and Elimination of Disruptive Classroom Behavior by Systematically Varying Teacher's Behavior," *Journal of Applied Behavior Analysis*, I (1968), 35-45.

Unit 6 • Exercise 1

Fill in the blanks with the right word. Refer to the text for correct answers as often as necessary.

1. In one first grade when teachers said "sit down" more often the children _____ _____ more.

2. "Sit down" follows the child's response of standing up. If as a result standing up occurs more often, then "sit down" must be acting as a _____.

3. "Sit down" is also a _____ for the child's response of sitting down.

4. Since sitting down follows the signal quite quickly and the increase in standing up may not be noted by the teacher, the teacher may be trapped into thinking that saying "sit down" _____.

5. The teacher's words are having the _____ effect from that intended.

6. The parent who tries to teach her child mainly by scolding rather than praising is likely to get caught in the _____ trap.

7. She is _____ for scolding because it seems to work. Her child is likely to _____ his misbehavior for awhile.

8. The very same behavior she does not want will be _____.

9. Peter got most of his ——————————— from his mother for misbehaving.

10. Peter's mother taught him to misbehave by ——————— to misbehavior and not ——————————— good behavior.

11. Only when his mother clearly rewarded Peter for good behavior did he get ———————————.

12. If a parent is using rewards and praise for good behaviors, then a little ——————————— will not hurt.

13. It is only when the main way in which a child gets ——————————— from adults is through criticism that we run into the criticism trap.

14. To escape the criticism trap the teacher must establish conditions which permit her to ——————————— more and ——————————— less.

15. Three conditions may be needed to change a parent's behavior. First, cues or ——————————— to praise more are needed; second, one needs to get praising going through practice; third, a way must be found to get ——————————— for praising more.

16. A parent can learn to praise more by making a rule. When I give out ———————————, I tell my child what I liked that he was doing. The tokens serve as a ——————————— to praise.

17. To use this procedure the parent only needs a supply of ——————————— to pass out and some payoff when they are turned back in.

18. Putting up ――――――――――― is another way to re-mind yourself to praise more and criticize less.

19. Some parents need help in learning how to be good

――――――――――.

20. Like anyone else, a mother needs to receive

――――――――――― for praising if she is to learn to praise more often.

21. Sometimes reinforcement for a mother's praise behavior comes from improved behavior in her ―――――――――.

22. It might also come from her ―――――――――. She might even ask him to praise her for praising more.

23. Keeping a record of praise behavior can help to reinforce more ――――――――― by showing the mother that it is working.

Check your answers with those in the back of the book. Where you have made errors, study the unit again.

Unit 6 • Exercise 2

A STUDY OF PRAISING AND CRITICIZING BEHAVIOR

This is a two-week project. For the first week you will only be recording how often you praise. During the second week you will be using one of the methods described in this unit and the information in the next unit to increase your praise behavior.

A recording sheet is provided on the page following this exercise.

Steps to take:
1. DEFINE THE BEHAVIORS TO BE COUNTED.
   We want you to count praise comments and critical comments.

   PRAISE
   COMMENTS: Any statements of affection, approval, interest, or praise directed to a child, your husband, the family, the children. Examples: "good job," "thanks," "nice," "great," "well done," "I'm proud of you," "that's interesting."

   CRITICAL
   COMMENTS: Any statements of complaint, criticism, wrong-doing, such as: "no," "don't," "cut it out," "wrong," "stop that," "grow up," "act your age," "don't be silly," "smart alec," "bad boy," "what did you do now?"

2. DECIDE HOW TO COUNT THEM.
   Possible methods:
   A. Have a paper and pencil beside you at the dinner table and make a mark after P or after C each time they occur.
   B. Instruct your husband to count them for you. A high school aged child could also do this with practice.
   C. Borrow a tape recorder. Tape dinner time and count it later.

3. DECIDE ON A TIME AND PLACE.
   Try to pick a period each day when you are interacting with your children for at least ten minutes. Count your praise and criticism each day for the same period of time, ten minutes,

fifteen minutes, or twenty minutes. We would suggest dinner time as a good possibility. You are free to choose another time.

4. RECORD EACH DAY YOUR COUNTS ON THE REPORT FORM (next page). Graph the results.

5. BRING YOUR RESULTS TO THE NEXT GROUP MEETING (if you are working with a group.)

(The next instructions for this project are provided with Unit 7.)

REPORT FORM

NAME _____

TIME OF DAY _____

ACTIVITY _____

DATE	PRAISE	CRITICISM	DATE	PRAISE	CRITICISM
1.			8.		
2.			9.		
3.			10.		
4.			11.		
5.			12.		
6.			13.		
7.			14.		

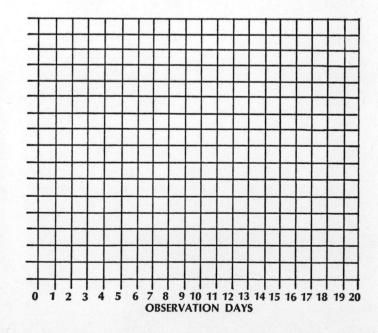

NUMBER OF PRAISE COMMENTS = X
NUMBER OF CRITICAL COMMENTS = 0

0 1 2 3 4 5 6 7 8 9 10 11 12 13 14 15 16 17 18 19 20
OBSERVATION DAYS

Unit 7
HOW TO REINFORCE

Using reinforcers effectively is a skillful art. Somehow, by the way in which you behave, you have to get those around you to like you and behave to please you rather than behaving because they are afraid of you. We believe there are two big steps on the road to being a successful reinforcer of other people.

STEP 1 involves getting out of the criticism trap. This may require lots of practice with new ways of reacting in situations where you have used criticism in the past. *You must take the role of an actor playing at being a positive parent until you are that parent.* In this unit we provide some materials and exercises to increase your skills in using *social reinforcers* and *activity reinforcers*. These materials and exercises can be helpful in learning to escape the criticism trap. Remember also that token reinforcers can be used to deal with many problems and to cue praising.

STEP 2 involves learning to communicate emotionally* with children while giving reinforcers. Reinforcers can be used in such a way that we can get a child to behave, but at the same time we may convey the attitude that we don't care about the child. For example, it is possible to use candy rewards to get a child to make his bed and still convey to the child that you don't like him. "So, you got it done. Here's your candy bar."

Social reinforcers, activity reinforcers, and token reinforcers can be used skillfully or they can be *misused*. When reinforcers are used skillfully, one hardly even notices they are being used.

---

communicate emotionally: Letting children know you care for *them* and are interested in *them* as you teach them.

Social reinforcers

Social reinforcers include words of praise, expressions, nearness, and physical contact. The first step in learning to be a good social reinforcer is to identify, study, and practice a *variety* of ways of producing potential social reinforcers.

POSSIBLE PRAISING WORDS AND PHRASES

Good

That's right

Excellent

That's clever

Exactly

Good job

Good thinking

Thank you

I'm pleased with that

Great

Groovy

I like that

I love you

That's interesting

That shows a great deal of work

You really pay attention

You should show this to your father

Show Grandma your picture

(Said to Father at dinner) Jimmy got right down to work after
    school and his homework is done already.

That was very kind of you

EXPRESSIONS

Smiling

Winking

Nodding up and down

Looking interested

Laughing

Clapping

NEARNESS

Walking together

Sitting on Linda's bed

Talking and listening to each other

Eating together

Playing games with your child

PHYSICAL CONTACT

Touching

Hugging

Sitting in lap

Patting head, shoulder, or back

Stroking arm

Shaking hand

Holding hand

MAKING PRAISE WORK

Dr. Haim Ginott, author of *Between Parent and Child,* has nicely pointed out that too often what we consider to be praise is not reacted to by the child as such. Just think how often someone has said to you *how great you are* when you really felt nothing of the sort. Take a child who has been repeatedly told he is stupid and who has failed often. He is not likely to jump with joy when a parent tells him, "You are smart." The praise words do not fit with his own feelings. On the other hand, if this same child has been working hard for twenty minutes to complete ten long division problems for homework and they were all done correctly when his mother checked them, he might believe a statement like this: "I saw you working hard on your arithmetic for twenty minutes. Every one of them is right and, you know, your writing is really neat and clear." These words simply *describe* what the child did and show appreciation* by the *detailed attention the parent gives to the child's work or behavior.* Ginott says it's usually better to make praise *descriptive* rather than *judging*.

The less you know about a child the more likely descriptive praise will be effective and judging praise will miss the mark. However, it is also possible to make judging words such as, "Good," "Great," "That's clever" effective for children by initially pairing such words with descriptions of what the child did to earn such praise. *Praise the behavior, not the whole child.*

"Jimmy ate all the meat and carrots on his plate. That's good eating."

"Mary sat quietly through the whole church service. She's a good listener."

MAKE PRAISE DESCRIPTIVE.
PRAISE THE BEHAVIOR, NOT THE WHOLE CHILD.

"Aaron, you kept at that one for a long time and you finally got it. That's good working. When we work hard, we learn."

By providing, again and again, clear examples of what is good working, good listening, good talking, good responding, good thinking, or being cooperative, we teach children what we mean by such praise statements. Later, when we say briefly "good listening," "good talking," "good boy," or "You're a good eater," they are no longer empty words.

Simply describing what a child does or did that you like is the first step to good praising. Tying such descriptions to short

---

appreciation: Liking for something or someone.

---

praise words is the next step. Finally, one can use a mixture of short words, or gestures, to signify approval or correctness, mixed in with more detailed description of praiseworthy behaviors.

Activity Reinforcers

Any preferred activity can be used to reinforce a less preferred activity. Next to the use of praise, the use of reinforcing activities is the most readily available motivating tool the parent has. Yet so often, as Gwendolyn did, the parent throws them away, or gives them away for free.

Often we want to teach children the general rule that "Learning more grown-up behaviors has a payoff." The parent does this by constantly talking about new examples of this general rule. For example, "Toni finished her dinner today; you can help Mother serve the dessert." "Jeff, you really improved in your report card grades; why don't you decide what we should have for dinner tonight." Instead of just telling a child he can go play, or instead of just saying it is time for lunch, *set it up so that the child has earned a privilege by behaviors he has learned which please you.*

USE ACTIVITIES THE CHILDREN LIKE
AS REWARDS FOR DESIRED BEHAVIORS.

POSSIBLE ACTIVITY REINFORCERS (PRIVILEGES)

Going first
Running errands
Helping clean up
Taking care of pets
Telling a joke at dinner
Playing house
Performing for parents
Making cookies or candy
Helping make dinner
Swinging
Outdoor camping
Getting to stay up late

Seeing a movie
Watching TV
Listening to music
Playing games with friends
Playing games with parents
Having a party
Making puppets and a
    puppet show
Doing art work related to
    studies
Making construction projects
Going on field trips

Having a friend stay overnight
Being thrown around in a
    circle by Daddy
Choosing songs to sing
Singing songs
Reading to Mother
Coloring Easter Eggs
Going shopping
Eating

Spending special time with
    Mother
Getting to make puzzles
Going out to play
A trip to Kiddie Land
Decorating a Christmas tree
Studying with a friend
Getting to read a new book
Being read to

How to use reinforcers and how not to

Social and activity reinforcers can be used meaningfully and they can be used in ways which fail to communicate what you want a child to learn and feel.

For each of the following, mark the parent response (A or B) you think does the best job of reinforcing. Then read the comments.

EXAMPLE 1
Jimmy has been well behaved at the dinner table.

A.   **FATHER:**   "My, what a good boy you've been during dinner tonight."

B.   **FATHER:**   "Let's see, who gets the wishbone? Jimmy, you've shown good manners tonight. I'm going to give this one to you."

Comments: Jimmy might react to A with "Does he mean I'm not usually a good boy? I'll show him that I'm not." B is specific in praising "good manners," and uses a trivial but fun reinforcer in addition.

EXAMPLE 2
When called in the morning, Mary dressed quickly and came downstairs for breakfast, but she forgot to wash her hands.

A.   **MOTHER:**   "My you were quick this morning. Breakfast is almost ready. Your dress looks pretty, Mary. I like that yellow."

      MARY: "So do I, Mommy."

      MOTHER: "Did you wash your hands and face?"

      MARY: "Oh, I forgot. Be right back." *She goes to wash.*

B. **MOTHER:** "Mary, let me see your hands. You forgot to wash, didn't you?"

MARY: "But they're not dirty."

MOTHER: "Go wash them and your face, too."

Comments: In *A* Mother started by praising the things Mary did right. Then she reminded Mary of what she had forgotten. Mary's attitude was accepting. Mary felt her mother liked her. In *B* Mother criticized Mary and Mary resisted.

EXAMPLE 3

It's almost bedtime and Billy has his cars and roads (wooden blocks) spread all over the living room. Billy is intent in his play.

A. **MOTHER:** [*Getting on the floor and entering into Billy's play,*] "My car can stay right on this road and go over this bridge."

BILLY: "I have to stop for gas here." [*Billy goes through all the steps of putting gas into the car.*] "Zoom, Zoom, I'm on the way to the circus to see the lions."

MOTHER: "Billy, it's nearly bedtime. In the next few minutes I want you to put your cars and blocks away and get your pajamas on. When you're all ready, I have a special treat for you."

Billy asks what it is, but Mother says it's a surprise . . . . Billy returns ready for bed in less than five minutes. He finds two chocolate-covered graham crackers and a glass of milk waiting for him. He smiles.

MOTHER: "You surprised *me* by doing all those things so fast."

B. **MOTHER:** "Billy, put your things away and get ready for bed and I'll read you a story."

BILLY: [*whining*] "Just five more minutes?"

MOTHER: "No, I said now. You do it now."

BILLY: "All————————right."

He pouts and fusses as he throws his blocks and cars into a box and dawdles his way to the bedroom.

Comments: Because Billy was intently involved in play, in *A* Mother showed understanding* of his involvement* by entering into his play and by giving him five minutes to bring it to an end. She then used a strong reinforcer (a surprise) to counter his play interest and motivate Billy to get ready for bed. In *B*, the story was not a strong enough reinforcer to make Billy want to quit playing.

EXAMPLE 4

It's time for bed and Kenny wants to watch TV some more. He's just started watching a new show.

A. **MOTHER:** "I should have caught you before this one started. I'll tell you what. You hurry and get on your pajamas and then you can decide whether you want to finish watching this show or have a story, but you have to be in bed ready for sleep by eight o'clock."

Kenny races for the bedroom as the first commercial comes on.

B. **MOTHER:** "Kenny, get ready for bed now or no story tonight."

KENNY: "Oh, Mom. I want to see the Hillbillies."

FATHER: "You heard what your mother said. Now get going."

Kenny trudges off, stamping his feet.

Comments: Again, Mother recognized Kenny's involvement with other reinforcers and used this to get Kenny ready for bed with little difficulty. By giving Kenny a choice of the TV reinforcer or a story, but not both, Mother solved two problems. Kenny got his TV reinforcer, and Mother got Kenny to bed on time. Very often *giving a choice* is an important step in making reinforcers work. In *B*, Mother set her consequence up as a threat and failed to recognize the strong TV reinforcer. At that point, Father could only step in and make the threat stick. Kenny went to bed unhappy.

---

involvement: Intense attention to something.

understanding: To know about.

EXAMPLE 5

Margaret, ten, forgot to make her bed this morning. She had been forgetting* quite regularly lately.

A. MOTHER: "Margaret, hurry up and make your bed before the school bus comes or you'll just have to miss it and walk to school and be late."

MARGARET: [*Starting to cry*] "But Mother, there isn't enough time. I don't want to be late." [*She is very upset*].

MOTHER: "Okay for today, but *don't* you dare forget tomorrow."

B. MOTHER: "Listen Margaret. You have been forgetting to make your bed quite a bit lately. Let's try something else to help you remember. The movie about "Big Red" you want to see is coming next weekend. I'll put a sign by the door of your room that says 'Make Bed' to remind you, *and* if you don't forget for the next five days, I'll take you to that movie."

MARGARET: "I'll really try, Mother. I'd like to see "Big Red" with you."

Comments: In *A* Mother set up a conflict situation. There might not be enough time to make the bed and catch the bus. The consequence was punishment for Margaret. She got upset and Mother gave in. In *B* Mother decided that Margaret could use a stronger reinforcer. She thought of something really important to Margaret, a movie about a dog. *Important rewards help us remember.* Finally, she let the bed go for that morning. Getting to school was also very important to both of them.

EXAMPLE 6

Buzz has been dawdling and will be late for the school bus unless he hurries with breakfast.

A. MOTHER: "Buzz, you've got two minutes left for breakfast before you must leave for the bus. If you hurry and finish you won't have to leave home so hungry."

---

forgetting: Not remembering.

B. **MOTHER:** "Hurry and finish your breakfast and you can be on time for the bus."
Buzz dawdles on and misses the bus. Mother is angry and punishes him by making him stay in all day. They are both "fit to be tied" by evening.

Comments: In *A* Mother knows she should not give Buzz the choice of missing the bus because he might prefer that choice. The choice she gave him, therefore, was eat faster or miss part of breakfast. She figured being a little hungry this morning might motivate him to eat faster tomorrow. So it was all right if he missed part of his breakfast this morning. In *B*, needless to say, Mother guessed wrong in setting up her choices.

EXAMPLE 7
Ruby fixes breakfast for her younger sister and brother without being asked.
A. **MOTHER:** "How nice. What a grown-up girl. You are an angel."
B. **MOTHER:** "Ruby, you are such a good helper to me. You set out their glasses and cereal bowls and filled them without spilling. Your brother and sister must appreciate having a sister like you."

Comments: In *A* the praise is to the person and not to the behavior. As a *person* Ruby is a little worried about being grown-up, and she knows she's not an angel. She cringed a little during her mother's praise. In *B*, Mother showed appreciation by describing the nice things she had done.

EXAMPLE 8
Joanne sets the table when asked to do so by her mother.
A. **MOTHER:** "That looks very pretty, Joanne, to see a table set so nicely. You even remembered that all of the forks go on the left. Thank you."
B. **MOTHER:** "You are a darling to be such a good helper. Let me give you a hug."
Joanne pulls away as Mommy tries to hug her.

Comments: In *A* Mother used descriptive praise. She described what Joanne had done which she appreciated. In *B*,

Mother acted as if Joanne's behavior were an act of deep love and affection. All the time she was setting the table, Joanne was worrying about what Mother would do when she found Joanne had torn her brand-new dress. When you praise the *person*, rather than the behavior, there is a good chance the person will not accept it, because he is not always "good," "kind," "loving," or "an angel." When you praise the behavior, you do not have this problem.

EXAMPLE 9
Kathy packed her own lunch and is ready for school on time.
A. **MOTHER:** "Kathy, you forgot to put away the mayonnaise, but I love you for being such a good helper this morning."
B. **MOTHER:** "Kathy, you sure got your day off to a good start. You got dressed and ready for school ahead of time and even packed your own lunch. That's pretty good for a ten-year-old girl. As a special treat, why don't you buy some cupcakes for your lunch on the way to school."
Mother gives Kathy twelve cents.

Comments: In *A* Mother starts by criticizing after Kathy had done such a good job. Kathy was hurt and didn't respond to the statement about being a good helper. Mother should have turned it around and *praised first*, been more specific about what Kathy did right, and then reminded her to please put the mayonnaise away too. In *B* Mother was descriptive in her praise and added a special treat that was appropriate for a girl who fixed her own lunch.

The next series of examples simply focus on some good ways to handle a variety of situations. Later (Exercise 4) you will be asked to specify why the different things which were done by Mother or Father are examples of good training.

EXAMPLE 10
Jonathan is supposed to practice the piano. He has been taking lessons only six weeks. He finds it hard work, because he is not yet skillful.

MOTHER: "I think you need some help in learning to practice. Suppose we try this. We'll make a chart showing how much you practice each day. For each minute of practice up to thirty minutes you earn points. Now what can we spend points for?"

· · · · · ·

Mother suggests staying up an extra half hour on Saturday, a fishing trip with Dad, and so on.

MOTHER: "For right now, you practice for ten minutes and then we can make some oatmeal cookies together."

Jonathan decided to start earning points to go fishing. He practiced fifteen minutes before coming to Mother to help make cookies. Since the fishing trip was off in the future, Mother decided that making cookies right now might help get things going in a positive way. It sure beats nagging!

EXAMPLE 11
Bill grabs for the meat at dinner without asking for it to be passed.

Instead of scolding or slapping his hand, Mother ignored it for now.

FATHER: [*Two minutes later*] "Please pass the meat."

MOTHER: "That's good manners, Father, to ask to have the meat passed like that. You set a good example for the children."

Bill noted what Mother said, appreciated the fact that she hadn't scolded him, and was careful next time to ask that the bread and jam be passed to him. Mother was then able to praise Bill for good manners.

EXAMPLE 12
Ginger's report card shows improved grades in three subjects.

FATHER: "Hey, Ginger, that's really something. You went from a Satisfactory to Excellent in Reading, from Satisfactory to Excellent in Social Studies, and from Poor to Satisfactory in Arithmetic. That's an improvement in *three* subjects at once. You must have been really working to earn that." *He gives her a hug.*

EXAMPLE 13

Henry, six, has been practicing hitting a baseball with his dad. He has shown improvement. This last time out he hit more than half of the balls thrown to him.

FATHER: [*On the way in*] "You know there was a time I wasn't sure you were going to get it and learn how to meet the ball. But, wow, you sure have improved. You must have hit more than half of my pitches today, and I had to chase a couple of them clear down to that fire hydrant. You're coming along. You stay with it and you'll be a good ball player." *Henry grins and sort of struts in holding his dad's hand.*

EXAMPLE 14

Bob and Linda go the whole day without teasing each other or fighting.

MOTHER: [*To Father at dinner*] "Bob and Linda have been so cooperative with each other today, I think maybe we should play some games with them tonight. Kids, do you want to play some games after dinner?"

BOB: "I want to play Spoons."

LINDA: "And I want to play Yahtzee."

MOTHER: "We have time to play them both."

EXAMPLE 15

Marie offers to do the dishes tonight without being asked.

MOTHER: "You sure know how to please me. I'll remember to do you a special favor that will please you too."

Summary

1. *Learning how to reinforce involves:*
   A. *Getting out of the criticism trap by learning positive ways of handling situations in which you were critical in the past.*
   B. *Learning to use reinforcers in ways which assure the children that you are fond of them and like them.*

2. *Most children are (or can be taught to be) responsive to praise, affection, and other social reinforcers. The parent needs to know a variety of ways of telling or showing children they are doing well.*

3. *There are a host of activities which are reinforcing for children. The parent needs to know about these and how to use them as reinforcers.*

4. *In using praise to reinforce behavior, one should describe, not judge; praise the behavior, not the person as a whole.*

5. *There are a large number of everyday events such as eating, playing, and going places which can be used by the parent to reinforce desired behaviors in children. The parent needs to get in the habit of using these events as consequences for desired behaviors.*

6. *If you must remind a child of a misbehavior, find something to praise first. This leaves little doubt about your liking for him. He is ready to listen to you.*

7. *When a child is involved in an activity, allow some time to plan an ending. This avoids many battles. Also try to make the new activity as reinforcing as possible. Focus on the positive.*

8. *Giving a choice between alternatives* acceptable to Mother is one way of ruling out alternatives unacceptable to Mother without seeming to be punishing.*

---

alternatives: Letting the child choose between two things he can do.

Unit 7 • Exercise 1

Place one word in each blank. Return to the unit as needed.

1. The effective use of reinforcement involves _____ big steps.

2. The first step involves getting out of the_____ trap.

3. Escaping the criticism trap may involve lots of_____ in new ways of reacting to old situations.

4. You must take the role of an actor playing at being a _____ parent until you are that parent.

5. The second step in becoming an effective reinforcer involves learning to _____ emotionally with children while giving reinforcers.

6. By communicating emotionally with children, we mean showing them that you _____ for them, are interested in them, and like them, at the same time you are _____ them things that they need to learn.

7. When _____ are used skillfully, one hardly notices they are being used.

8. _____ reinforcers are learned reinforcers which involve behavior such as tone of voice, words of praise, giving attention, being near, smiling, touching, etc.

9. Haim Ginott recommends that praise be _____ rather than judging.

10. Descriptive praise focuses on the details of behavior the parent wishes to ―――――――――.

11. ―――――――― praise is especially important in situations where you know little about what pleases a child.

12. "Jimmy, you ate all the meat and carrots on your plate," is an example of ―――――――― praise.

13. "You're smart, Jake" is an example of ―――――――― praise.

14. Any preferred activity can be used to reinforce a ―――――――― preferred activity.

15. As Gwendolyn did, the parent often gives away or throws away her ――――――――.

16. Often we want to teach children the general rule that "learning more grown-up behaviors has a――――――――."

17. Instead of just telling a child he can go play, or instead of just saying it is time for lunch, set it up so that the child has ―――――――― a privilege by behaviors he has learned which please you.

18. When reminding a child about something he forgot to do, it is better to first praise him for things he has done right and then to give the ――――――――. The child's attitude will be more accepting.

19. When a child is involved in play, the understanding parent allows some ―――――――― for the child to bring the play to an end.

20. It is also a good idea to make the new activities seem as reinforcing as possible to counter his play interest. Billy's mother did this by promising a _____.

21. Kenny's mother used the very activity (TV) Kenny was involved with to _____ his getting ready for bed quickly.

22. Giving a choice is often an important step in making reinforcers work. Kenny was given a choice between TV and his _____ story.

23. Mother A gave Buzz a choice between eating faster or or missing part of his _____.

24. Mother B gave Buzz a choice between eating faster or missing the school _____.

25. The best decision in giving Buzz a choice was made by Mother A or B (circle).

26. In setting up choices, it is important not to create impossible conflicts. Margaret's mother A created a conflict by setting up a choice between making her bed and catching the bus when there was not enough _____ for both.

27. Praise should be directed to the behavior rather than the _____.

28. When you praise the person, rather than the behavior, there is a good chance the person will not accept it, because he is not _____ "good," "kind," "loving," or "an angel."

29. If you have a criticism to make, it is a good idea to find something to ———————————— first. This leaves little doubt about your liking for the person you are correcting.

Check your answers with those in the back of the book. Where you have made errors, study the unit again.

Unit 7 • Exercise 2

Make a list of Praise Words and Phrases which you would be comfortable using.

1. _____
2. _____
3. _____
4. _____
5. _____
6. _____
7. _____
8. _____
9. _____
10. _____
11. _____
12. _____
13. _____
14. _____
15. _____
16. _____
17. _____
18. _____
19. _____
20. _____

Unit 7 • Exercise 3

Make a list of Reinforcing Activities available to use with your children.

1. _____
2. _____
3. _____
4. _____
5. _____
6. _____
7. _____
8. _____
9. _____
10. _____
11. _____
12. _____
13. _____
14. _____
15. _____
16. _____
17. _____
18. _____
19. _____
20. _____

Unit 7 • Exercise 4

For each of the examples of using reinforcers given on pages 108 to 110, tell in what ways the procedure is an example of the summary points about how to reinforce given on pages 110-111.

1. Jonathan and the piano.

   _____

   _____

   _____

   _____

2. Bill and grabbing for food.

   _____

   _____

   _____

3. Ginger's report card.

   _____

   _____

   _____

   _____

4. Henry and baseball.

   _____

   _____

   _____

   _____

5. Bob and Linda have a good day.

_____

_____

_____

_____

6. Marie volunteers for dishes.

_____

_____

_____

_____

Unit 7 • Exercise 5

INTRODUCING A PROCEDURE TO INCREASE PRAISE AND REDUCE CRITICAL COMMENTS

A continuation of project from Unit 6.

By now, you should be completing seven days of recording your behavior using one of the procedures presented in Unit 6. You should also have determined the behaviors to be recorded, method of recording, and the time of recording. You are now ready to complete the program.

STEPS TO TAKE:
1. SELECT one of the change procedures from Unit 6 discussed on pages 88 to 91.
2. WRITE OUT below your change plan and begin to follow it during the time when you are recording your praise behavior.
3. BRING YOUR RESULTS to the next group session.

CHANGE PLAN
Describe in outline the procedure to be used to increase praise and decrease criticism.

_____

_____

_____

_____

_____

_____

_____

_____

Unit 8

**PUNISHMENT: WHEN TO, HOW TO, AND
WHY NOT TO, USUALLY**

What is punishment?

Events which occur following behaviors and weaken the future
rate of such behaviors are called *punishers*. Gwendolyn encoun-
tered a variety of punishing events in getting ready for work. The
floor was cold when she stepped on it, the door frame hurt when
she walked into it, and the shower was freezing at first. Much of
our moment-to-moment traveling through space has been learned
because we were punished in the past. In general, we learn not
to make responses which are punished, and we learn to try other
responses which are not punished. When we as human beings
control consequent events to weaken the behavior of others, we
talk about the process as *punishment*.

There is probably no other area in the psychology of behavior where more emotion, confusion, and misunderstanding
have been generated than over the topic of punishment. Teachers
and parents have been told that they should not use punishment
because it doesn't work. It supposedly only produces temporary
effects. Some people believe that any use of punishment under
any circumstances is immoral. Some believe it is all right to punish
children severely as long as you don't slap them in the face. Some
equate any form of isolation procedure with prison, failing to be
concerned with the benefits to the child. Some believe we should
ban the word from the English language, as if that would somehow make people more loving.

Does punishment work?

The answer is "*Yes.*" There are many consequences which can be
shown to weaken behavior. The belief that punishment does not

work arises from observations that when punishment is stopped the punished behavior returns. When punishment is used, the punished behavior is less frequent, but after the punishment is removed, the punished behavior returns. But the same is true of reinforcement and no one questions whether it works. As long as a behavior is reinforced, it occurs at a high rate. When reinforcement is removed, the rate decreases. Both reinforcement and punishment work. They are sort of opposites of each other.

Most of the rules about reinforcers also apply to punishment, except we are talking about *weakening* rather than *strengthening* behavior. Punishment is more effective when it is immediate, as is reinforcement. Punishment is more effective when it is intense or given in greater quantity, as is reinforcement. The effects of punishment last longer when punishment is unpredictable and intermittent, just as with reinforcement.

There is no question that it is possible to use punishment to produce strong and lasting effects on behavior. *However, that doesn't mean we should do so.* Other matters need to be considered in deciding about when and where to use punishment.

Is the use of punishment immoral?

Some believe that hurting children in any way is evil. The advocates of unconditional love for children are often from the mental health professions, where they have rightfully learned that many of the problems people have stem from cruel treatment by other people or a deprived environment. Rightfully, they see the need for much positive care in helping such persons.

But consider this:
A child has been kept tied down in a bed whenever he has to be left alone (nighttime, for example) to prevent the child from digging into his flesh and cutting a blood vessel. Suppose now that by applying a mild electric shock (no more painful than a doctor's needle) every time the child begins to hurt himself, we could get rid of this behavior in three days. What is the moral thing to do: to use punishment to get rid of a behavior which has completely restricted this child's chances for a normal life, or to cuddle him and be kind to him each time he begins to hurt himself? Mothers have little trouble making such a choice.

122

Remember Peter?

His mother punished him by placing him in his room with the door closed until he was quiet for five minutes. She used this only six times the first week and his behavior changed greatly. Positive responses to Mother increased after his demanding and aggressive behaviors were punished. Did the result justify the methods used?

Punishment does work and can be used to change undesired behaviors. When the long-term effects from the use of punishment lead to far more good than the failure to use punishment, the moral person will do what is best for the child and use punishment. It would be immoral *not* to do everything possible to help children learn what is needed to live freely in our society. There are few mothers of two-year-olds who question the use of punishment when necessary to keep their child from being hurt or killed by automobiles, knives, gas, or fire.

The use of punishment, *per se,* is not immoral, even though punishment may be used in ways which are harmful to children or adults.

Why is punishment to be avoided, usually?

Punishment involves presenting aversive* consequences (a spanking) or *withdrawing* reinforcing consequences (taking away dessert, placing a child away by himself). We usually avoid physical punishment such as hitting children, not because it can't be made to work, but because it causes results we do not want. As parents and teachers, we want to teach children to come to us when they need help, have problems, and the like. This goal is inconsistent with a major effect of punishment, namely, *we learn to avoid* and escape* from those who punish us.* Here are some avoidance behaviors* and escape behaviors* we *teach children:*

aversive:	Consequences which usually hurt. Touching a hot stove, a spanking, getting hit by a car, being made fun of, and so on.
avoid:	To stay away from.
escape:	To get away from.
avoidance behaviors:	Behaviors which involve staying away from getting punished.
escape behaviors:	Behaviors which involve getting away from punishers.

CHEATING: avoiding the punishment that goes with being wrong.

TRUANCY: avoiding or escaping the many punishments which go with school failure, poor teaching, punitive administration of school.

RUNNING AWAY: (from home) escaping the many punishments parents can use.

LYING: avoiding the punishment that follows doing something wrong.

SNEAKING: avoiding being caught "misbehaving."

HIDING: avoiding being caught.

A MODEL FOR AGGRESSION

Another reason for avoiding the use of physical forms of punishment is that they show a child how to be aggressive to others. Children imitate* or model what they see adults doing. Children whose parents show much aggression towards them in the form of punishment are more aggressive with other children.

How does one use punishment effectively?

When we punish children, we teach negative attitudes (hate and fear) toward the punishing person, as well as teaching the child to avoid us in the future. Therefore, effective punishment must do at least four things:

1. Prevent avoidance and escape from the punisher.
2. Undo or prevent teaching the child a hateful attitude towards the punisher.
3. Reduce the need for punishment later.
4. Not provide a model of aggressive behavior.

Peter's mother used punishment effectively. She eliminated his objectionable behavior while improving the love between Peter and herself. Let's look at what she did in view of the four points just listed.

---

imitate: Doing as you see someone else do. Also called modelling.

---

1. **PREVENTING AVOIDANCE AND ESCAPE FROM THE PUNISHER**

Instead of spanking Peter, which might drive him away from her, Mother put Peter in his room where he could no longer get attention from her. This is a form of punishment consisting of taking away reinforcers. By taking away reinforcers (attention, in this case), Mother made it so Peter had to come back to her to get reinforcement. Furthermore, Mother has not been paired with strong, painful, or fear-producing punishers. Peter was ready to return to Mother as a reinforcer, rather than as a punisher to be feared.

Generally, taking away reinforcers as a punishment can be effective *as long as there are clear-cut steps provided for earning the reinforcers back*. Peter could earn his mother's attention back by being quiet for five minutes.

Taking away reinforcers for awhile provides one way to get around the problem posed by avoidance and escape behaviors. Another way to get around the problem is to be sure that the child cannot escape the punisher. This is only possible with very young children or in prisons. The parent seldom has this kind of control with older children and should therefore usually avoid all physical punishment. Also this approach can produce strong fears.

2. **UNDOING OR PREVENTING A HATEFUL ATTITUDE TOWARD MOTHER**

Undoing possible hate

Peter's mother gave Peter much attention and affection for cooperative behaviors. Being with Mother was reinforcing and positive contacts with Mother were increased. Even if Peter did not like being alone in his room, he did like being with his mother and Peter could make this happen by being quiet for five minutes.

Preventing hate

Peter's mother did two things to reduce resentment or hate from Peter. First, she punished by taking away reinforcers (Mother's attention) rather than by hitting him. Hate is built quickly and strongly when we punish by physically hurting someone. Peter's mother avoided this. Secondly, she did not get angry when punishing Peter. She remained calm while putting him in his room. Punishing in anger is likely to increase the hate feelings in the person being punished.

Thus, by not using physical punishment, and by not punishing in anger, Peter's mother was able to keep Peter's resentment at a low level. By being warm and praising for Peter's acceptable behaviors, she showed Peter that she really liked him, even if it was necessary to punish him at times.

3.   REDUCING THE NEED FOR LATER PUNISHMENT
Peter's mother did three things to reduce the need for later punishment.

A.   She gave a warning signal* before punishing Peter. Soon just warning Peter was enough to get him to behave. Saying "Stop that" had become a learned punisher because it was followed by punishment several times.

B.   She rewarded behaviors incompatible with his bad behaviors. Peter could receive lots of attention from Mother by being good. Peter was taught ways of getting his mother's attention that did not require him to be bad.

C.   She made sure that she did not reinforce Peter's objectionable behaviors. If the same behaviors are sometimes reinforced and sometimes punished, it is much more difficult to get rid of them.

Punishment is not needed when a child has learned to be good or when he has learned to stop misbehaving when given a gentle warning.

4.   DO NOT PROVIDE A MODEL OF AGGRESSIVE BEHAVIOR
Peter's mother also followed this rule in her choice of punishments.

---

warning signal: A learned punisher. A signal which has been closely followed by punishment and which indicates punishment might be coming. The parent gives a warning like "stop that," "don't," "no, no," before punishing. Later only the warning signal is necessary to stop a behavior.

RULES TO REMEMBER

1. **EFFECTIVE PUNISHMENT is given immediately.**

2. **EFFECTIVE PUNISHMENT relies on taking away reinforcers and provides a clear-cut method for earning them back.**

3. **EFFECTIVE PUNISHMENT makes use of a warning signal, usually words.**

4. **EFFECTIVE PUNISHMENT is carried out in a calm, matter-of-fact way.**

5. **EFFECTIVE PUNISHMENT is given along with much reinforcement for behaviors incompatible with the punished behavior.**

6. **EFFECTIVE PUNISHMENT is consistent. Reinforcement is not given for the punished behaviors.**

When should punishment be used?

There are three situations where punishment may be needed because reinforcement is likely to fail or be costly. These are:
1. When a problem behavior occurs *so often* there is no good behavior to reinforce.
2. When the nature or intensity of the problem behavior leads to serious *questions of safety* for the child or others.
3. When the use of reinforcement is not effective because other *more powerful reinforcers* are causing the problem behavior.

Let's consider examples of each of these situations.

HIGH RATE BEHAVIOR
We have worked with a few children where the only way they knew of interacting with other children was by hitting, pushing, or kicking. They did not know how to play. With such children, a warning followed by being placed in a room by themselves for a few minutes if they failed to stop hitting helped in reducing the aggression. But it was also necessary to teach such children how to play nicely—how to take turns, to share, and to win and lose. Otherwise it might have been necessary to keep using punishment forever.

QUESTIONS OF SAFETY

Earlier we gave the example of the child who dug into his own flesh and was punished with a mild shock to stop this behavior. The child might have killed himself before his behavior could have been changed by using rewards. Correctly used, punishment can train children quickly to stop certain behaviors.

It is important that a young child learn not to go into the streets until he can be taught to cross streets safely. A parent cannot afford to take the time to reward the child when he is not in the street and not reward him when he is in the street. A simple "No. We don't go into the streets," followed by one or two quick swats on the fanny can teach this lesson quickly. At the same time, the parent should reinforce staying out of the street.

A similar approach may be necessary with stoves, knives, poisons, matches, guns, and the like. For the very young child (under eighteen months) careful watching and keeping dangerous things away from him is the best route. When the child can understand words and is walking well, the child is safer if he has been taught to avoid such dangers. The key to teaching is to follow the rules for effective punishment given earlier, but use a brief physical punishment *following* the warning words.

For example, your child starts to reach for a pan of boiling water on the stove. Say, "No. Hot," and slap his hand quickly, or take his hand and briefly touch it to the side of the hot pan. Be careful to make it brief so as to avoid a burn.

Suppose you find your child on the kitchen floor with a sharp knife and a potato. Take the knife away. Say, "We don't play with knives. They can hurt us." Show him the knife. Put his hand out as if he were reaching for the knife, if he doesn't reach for it. Say, "No play," and give his outstretched hand a quick slap.

When you must use physical punishment, be smart about it. Make sure it teaches your child to AVOID THE DANGER, NOT YOU. Effective punishment is given IMMEDIATELY, uses a WARNING SIGNAL, is carried out in a CALM MANNER, and is specifically AIMED at a dangerous behavior you want to stop.

WHEN USING REINFORCERS IS INEFFECTIVE
(OR TOO MUCH TROUBLE)

Your six-year-old fails to come home from school on time. Warnings have done no good. It is important to you to know where your child is after school. On the way home she can get lots of reinforcement from other children as she stops here and there. You can't leave the house to fetch her each day because of the other children. So you make a rule. "For every minute after such and such a time you are late you will have to stay in from playing for five minutes (or you will lose five minutes of TV that night)." Take away so much of a fun time for so much lateness.

Four-year-old Billy likes to take toys away from his younger brother. This behavior is reinforced by having the toys to play with. To keep him from doing this, a warning followed by a short spank and time away from the toys for five to ten minutes is a beginning. Say, "You cannot take toys away from Clancy." (Swat, swat) "Give it back right now. You go into the living room and sit in the brown chair until I tell you you can play with these toys and Clancy, you are going to have to show me that you can share." The next step is to continue to teach what sharing is and to praise Billy for doing it.

More examples of how to punish the right way

EXAMPLE 1
Claire was a bright sixteen-year-old who was about to be expelled by her high school for being delinquent (truancy, poor grades, and "fighting" with her mother at home).[1]

What Was Done: At the time help was sought, Claire had been staying home, but was threatening to run away. There was no father in the home. Mother had taken away (as punishment) all money, use of telephone, and dating privileges. The treatment plan worked out with the mother and Claire was as follows: One note from school each day (saying that she attended all classes) earned Claire telephone privileges for that day. Four notes during the week earned one weekend date. Five notes earned two dates. This plan worked beyond belief even though Mother was very doubtful at first. Claire was punished by loss of privileges, but *she showed no change until a definite way to earn the privileges back (by showing responsible behavior) was provided.*

Comments: Peter earned back mother's attention by being quiet for five minutes. Claire earned back telephone and dating privileges by attending school regularly. Claire's plan worked so well that the notes could be stopped in a few months with no loss of attendance.

EXAMPLE 2

It's raining and Chuck comes in with mud all over his feet and starts across the kitchen floor tracking it up. He has been told to leave muddy shoes on the door rug.

MOTHER: [*In a matter-of-fact voice*] "Stop. Go back to the rug and take off your shoes. Here's a sponge to clean up your tracks. We'll clean the shoes when they're drier. Boy, it sure is wet out."

CHUCK: "Yeah, I know." *He gives an understanding smile.*

Comments: A similar approach can be taken to spilled milk.

EXAMPLE 3

Carol protests when asked to do dishes. Mother has been trying to get Carol to cheerfully accept some responsibilities at home and decides not to give up.

CAROL: "But, Mother, that is my favorite program. I don't want to miss it."

MOTHER: [*Getting the TV Guide*]. "Carol, you have had over thirty minutes since dinner to get the dishes done. You can take your choice. Do the dishes now and get to see at least part of this show and [*looking at the TV Guide*] your two other 'favorite shows' which follow this one, or we leave the TV off tonight."

Carol is still balky, but she does it and Mother has something to praise her for.

EXAMPLE 4

Jake is out playing with the boys. He is called for supper and does not come the first time.

	Mother called only once and served dinner, including Jake's portions. When he came in (ten minutes late), nothing was said. His food was cold and he could eat as he wanted to. Mother and Father talked to each other, to Jake, and to sister as if nothing was wrong.
JAKE:	"These potatoes are cold. I can't eat them."
MOTHER:	[Quietly] "If you come for dinner when I call you, your potatoes won't be cold."
	The next evening, Jake came in the first time he was called.
MOTHER:	"Thank you for coming so quickly. I like you to have a warm dinner, too."
	Jake smiled.

Comments: If Jake's mother had gone out to drag him in for dinner, that would be quite embarrassing in front of his friends. Holding dinner for him would reinforce being late. Calling many times would lead to Jake learning not to come the first time he is called.

EXAMPLE 5

Jan didn't get up when called. In the past Mother would call several times and then have to almost pull her out of bed. It was getting to be quite a drag for her mother. This time Mother called only once, was sure she got an "all right" response from Jan and did no more. Jan didn't come down until 8:30 and was late for school. She was upset.

MOTHER:	"I'm sorry you're late, but I called you and you answered. You are going to have to be responsible for getting you to school on time. Now hurry up and I'll give you a note saying you overslept."
	Later that day Mother bought an alarm clock for Jan. That evening she gave it to Jan.
MOTHER:	"Now you can take complete charge of getting up on time. If you are late, you will have no one to blame but you."
JAN:	"Hey, thanks. I've always wanted a clock of my own."

EXAMPLE 6

On the way home from school Tim gets into a fight with his friend Chuck. He comes in all dirty and a little bruised.

MOTHER:	[*Starting to clean Tim up*] "It looks like you lost. What happened?"

TIM:	"I got into a fight with Chuck. He called me a dirty name. He was mad 'cause I kept winning his marbles."
MOTHER:	"What did he look like? Was he hurt?"
TIM:	"Not really. Just dirty like me."
MOTHER:	"Well, I think you better go take a bath and put on different clothes."

Comments: Mother decided that Tim had already been punished enough so she didn't add to it. She also did not overly attend to his hurts.

EXAMPLE 7

Ernie won't go to sleep. He keeps getting out of bed and saying he can't sleep.

A. *The problem occurs every night. In the past, Mother has held him a little and gone into the bedroom with Ernie, rubbing his back awhile. She is now tired of all the extra work involved and wants to change his habits.*

> **MOTHER:** "Ernie, I want you to learn to go to bed and go right to sleep the first time. I've made this chart with spaces to cover the next two weeks. Each night you go to sleep without getting out of bed, I will place a star on your chart. When you get fourteen stars, we'll start looking for a puppy for you. Do you understand?"
>
> **ERNIE:** "Gee, I want a puppy. I'll try."
>
> **MOTHER:** "And one more thing, to help you learn and earn your stars we'll do one other thing. Your door can be open a little as long as you don't get out of bed. But if you get out of bed, the door is closed. Understand?"
>
> **Comments:** For children used to having a bedroom door open so they can see some light and hear the rest of the family, closing the door is punishment. Ernie might cry when this punishment is carried out, but his mother would have to stick to it. Changing habits of this sort takes only a few days, if you are consistent.

B. *Same problem, but this is the first time it has happened in quite a while.*

> **MOTHER:** "Let me get you a children's aspirin. That will help you sleep."

Mother gets him an aspirin and some water, has Ernie take them, and takes him back to bed. She comforts him a little and leaves.

Comments: It's not too important whether the aspirin really helps him get to sleep or not. The *idea* that he is being helped may be enough to relax him and allow him to sleep. A sugar pill might be just as effective.

Summary

Punishment is an effective method for changing behavior. However, because the person punished may learn to avoid and escape from the punisher, this is not usually a preferred method. There are problem behaviors where the use of punishment is the most humane thing that can be done. These problems usually involve very intense or very frequent problem behaviors. When punishment must be used, care must be taken to ensure its effectiveness and to minimize the development of avoidance behaviors. Effective punishment is given immediately. Effective punishment relies on withdrawal of reinforcers and provides clear steps for regaining them. Effective punishment makes use of a warning signal. Effective punishment is carried out in a calm, matter-of-fact way. Effective punishment is accompanied by much reinforcement for behavior incompatible with the behavior being punished. Effective punishment also uses procedures to make sure that undesired behaviors do not receive reinforcement.

NOTE TO UNIT 8
[1] G. L. Thorne, R.G. Tharp, and R.J. Wetzel, "Behavioral Modification Techniques: New Tools for Probation Officers," *Federal Probation*, XXXI (1967), 21-27.

Unit 8 • Exercise 1

1. Events which occur following behavior and weaken the future rate of such behaviors are called_____.

2. Punishment (does/does not) work.

3. Most of the rules about reinforcers apply to punishment, except we are talking about _____ rather than strengthening behavior.

4. Punishment is more effective when it is given

    _____.

5. Intense punishment is more effective in _____ behavior than less intense punishment.

6. The effects of punishment in weakening behavior last _____ when punishment is unpredictable and intermittent.

7. Just because punishment can be effective in changing behavior does _____ mean that we should use it.

8. In itself, use of punishment is not immoral or moral. Punishment should be used when the long-term effects from the use of punishment lead to more _____ than harm. Punishment should not be used when the long-term effects are more _____ than good.

9. We usually avoid physical punishment (such as hitting children) because it causes results we do not _____.

10. Children learn to _____ and escape from those who punish them.

11. When we avoid someone, we _____
_____ from them or try not to be near them.

12. When we escape from someone, we _____
_____ from them.

13. Hiding from Mother is an example of _____ behavior.

14. Running away from home is an example of _____ behavior.

15. Lying is an avoidance behavior since it attempts to prevent a _____ for misbehavior.

16. Cheating is an avoidance behavior which attempts to prevent the punishment for being _____.

17. Children imitate adult behaviors. They imitate the _____ behaviors of the punishing parent too.

18. To be effective, punishment must prevent avoidance and _____ from the punisher and minimize _____ reactions.

19. To be effective, the punisher must find ways to prevent teaching _____ toward the punisher.

20. To be effective, punishment must be carried out in ways which _____ the need for punishment later.

21. To be effective, the punisher should not provide a _____ of aggressive behavior.

22. Effective punishment is given _____.

23. Effective punishment relies on the taking away of _____, rather than applying painful consequences.

24. When reinforcers are taken away, effective punishment provides a _____ method for earning them back.

25. Effective punishment makes use of a _____ signal, usually in the form of words.

26. Effective punishment is carried out in a _____, matter-of-fact way.

27. Effective punishment is given along with much _____ for behaviors incompatible with the punished behavior.

28. Effective punishment is consistent. Reinforcement is _____ given for the punished behaviors.

29. Punishment may be necessary when a problem behavior occurs so often that there is no _____ behavior to reinforce.

30. Punishment may be necessary when there are serious questions of _____.

31. Punishment may be necessary when the _____ available are not strong enough, or it is too much trouble to deliver them.

32. Before Claire's mother got help, she had tried to punish Claire by taking away her reinforcers (telephone and dating privileges). She made the mistake of not providing Claire with a _____ way to earn them back.

Unit 8 • Exercise 2

For each of the examples of *How to punish the right way* on pages 129 to 133, point out in what ways the procedure used is an example of the Rules to Remember about *Effective Punishment*.

The Rules to Remember are as follows:
1. *Effective punishment* is given immediately.
2. *Effective punishment* relies on taking away reinforcers and provides a clear-cut method for earning them back.
3. *Effective punishment* makes use of a warning signal, usually words.
4. *Effective punishment* is carried out in a calm, matter-of-fact way.
5. *Effective punishment* is given along with much reinforcement for behaviors incompatible with the punished behavior.
6. *Effective punishment* is consistent. Reinforcement is not given for the punished behavior.

For each example below, the numbers 1 to 6 stand for the Rules to Remember above. If the example illustrates a given point, write in just how it does. We have done the first one to show you how.

EXAMPLE 1
Overcoming Claire's truancy.

1. <ins>Not illustrated.</ins>

2. <ins>Lost dating & telephone privileges; earned them back with notes proving she went to all classes.</ins>

3. <ins>Not illustrated.</ins>

4. <ins>Not illustrated.</ins>

5. She was rewarded for attending classes with dating and telephone privileges.
6. (Mother stuck to rules) This was not illustrated but did happen.

EXAMPLE 2
Chuck comes in all muddy.

1. _____
   _____

2. _____
   _____

3. _____
   _____

4. _____
   _____

5. _____
   _____

6. _____
   _____

EXAMPLE 3
Carol protests about dishes.

1. _____
   _____

2. _____
   _____

3. _____
   _____

4. _____

_____

5. _____

_____

6. _____

_____

EXAMPLE 4
Jake comes in late for dinner.

1. _____

_____

2. _____

_____

3. _____

_____

4. _____

_____

5. _____

_____

6. _____

_____

EXAMPLE 5
Jan did not get up when called.

1. _____

_____

2. _____

_____

3. _____

_____

4. _____

_____

5. _____

_____

6. _____

_____

(We skip 6 on purpose.)

EXAMPLE 7
Ernie won't go to sleep, Case A.

1. _____

_____

2. _____

_____

3. _____

_____

4. _____

_____

5. _____

_____

6. _____

_____

Now do the same thing for the following examples . . .

A. The case of Peter from Unit 1

1. _____
   _____
2. _____
   _____
3. _____
   _____
4. _____
   _____
5. _____
   _____
6. _____
   _____

B. The child reaching for the pan of boiling water. (Questions of Safety, page 128)

1. _____
   _____
2. _____
   _____
3. _____
   _____
4. _____
   _____
5. _____
   _____
6. _____
   _____

Unit 8 • Exercise 3

On the chart below, make daily notes of behaviors you punish your child for during the week. Summarize your notes into a list of the five behaviors you would like to change the most.

Behaviors I punished _____ for this week.

NOTES ON PUNISHMENT			
DAY	TIME	BEHAVIOR	PUNISHMENT

BEHAVIOR   PUNISHMENT

1. _____   1. _____

2. _____   2. _____

3. _____   3. _____

4. _____   4. _____

5. _____   5. _____

Unit 9

REASONS, RULES, AND REMINDERS

In the first eight units of this program we have provided many examples in which a variety of signals, words, or cues have been used to help get the desired behaviors going.

EXAMPLES OF SIGNALS AND WORDS
USED TO GET BEHAVIOR GOING
1.   Mrs. E. was instructed to make her *rules clear* so that the children knew what was expected of them.
2.   GRANDMA'S RULE gave a general procedure for instructing children about their chores or responsibilities. "You can go out and play, after you finish your chores."
3.   In teaching Lisa to learn to get ready for school by herself, Lisa's mother *talked* to her the night before *to remind her* about what was expected of her in the morning. She also laid out her clothes ahead of time to serve as a *reminder* as Lisa woke up.
4.   Teresa's mother made a *chart* with all the *rules* on it of how she could earn points.
5.   The two school token programs we summarized each spelled out to the children the *rules* for earning tokens.
6.   Mrs. James found that giving out tickets helped *remind* or cue herself to use more praise.
7.   In escaping the criticism trap, we suggested putting up *signs* to help remind you to praise.
8.   In rewarding or punishing children, we have nearly always given examples where the parent *tells the child* exactly what he did right or wrong. The child is given the *reason* for being rewarded and punished to help him learn a rule about what is expected of him.

If what is learned is what is reinforced (or punished), why all this focus on reasons, rules, and reminders? The answer has two parts.

1.   The complete rule about "what is learned" says: *The child learns to do, under a given set of conditions, what is reinforced.* We not only teach a child what to do, *but when to do it.* Reasons, rules, and reminders help the child learn *when* he is supposed to do *what; or,* in the case of punished behaviors, when he is not supposed to do what.

Examples specifying the **conditions** under which behavior is to occur:

1.   **In the classroom during work periods,** we are in our seats and paying attention.
2.   **When mother asks you to do the dishes,** you do the dishes.
3.   **When you are called to get up,** dress yourself quickly.
4.   **When the light is red,** we do not cross the street.
5.   **When the fire alarm rings,** we line up and go outside quietly.
6.   **When the sign says 35 MPH,** we do not drive faster than 35.

2.   Our longer range goal is to teach a child to guide his own behavior, make good decisions, reason clearly about choices and consequences, solve problems on his own, and plan ahead. When a child is taught the rules about consequences of his own behaviors, he can make better decisions for himself when his parents are not there.

For example, a child is taught to follow Grandma's Rule, "we work before we play." If he follows this rule in setting up the order in which he does things, he is more likely to become a good worker, than if he does not. He has also been taught the rule that "good workers earn more money and can have more reinforcers." Having been taught to follow these rules, a child is considered by others as responsible and a good citizen. He is more likely to enjoy the rewards available in our society.

Reasons and rules

By giving children reasons for our actions or their actions, we begin to teach them to "reason out" the consequences of their own behavior. When we reason, we talk to ourselves in our heads. Learning the words that connect what we do with the consequences allows the child to know in advance what the consequences will be and, therefore, make better choices.

IN TEACHING A CHILD TO USE REASONS, THE STEPS ARE THESE:

1. TELL YOUR CHILD WHAT HE DID THAT EARNED A REWARD, OR PUNISHMENT.
   A. "I am going to give you a treat because you did such a good job of cleaning your room."
   B. "You'll have to miss TV tonight because you did not come home from school when you were supposed to."

2. AFTER A CHILD HAS BEEN GIVEN MANY EXAMPLES OF REASONS FOR REINFORCEMENT OR REASONS FOR PUNISHMENT, BEGIN TO ASK HIM TO STATE THE REASONS.
   A. "Why do you suppose I'm going to give you a special treat tonight? What do you think you did to please me?"
   B. "You did a good job. What do you think might happen?"
   C. "I'm going to have to punish you. Tell me what you did wrong."
   D. "Why do you suppose you got hurt coming home today?"
   WHEN THE CHILD ANSWERS YOUR QUESTION, SAY THE WHOLE THING BACK TO HIM.
   A. "Yes, you've earned a special treat because you did such a good job of cleaning your room."
   B. "That's right, you didn't come home from school on time so you will have to miss TV tonight."
   C. "That's right, you fell down and got hurt because you were not looking where you were running."

3. WHEN YOUR CHILD IS ABLE TO TELL YOU REASONS FOR SPECIFIC BEHAVIOR, BEGIN TO WORK ON GENERAL RULES FOR BEHAVIOR.
   General rules about behavior are taught by showing your child how something that has happened is an example of a more general rule.
   A. "You did the dishes on time, so you will get to see your TV program. *When you do your chores, good things happen.*" (Or "Working hard has a payoff.")

B.   "You fell down and got hurt because you were not
     looking where you were running. *It's dangerous not to
     pay attention to where you are going.*"

C.   "I spanked you for running into the street. *If you run
     in the street, a car can hurt you.*"

D.   "You and Mary had a nice time together today. *When
     you are nice to her, she is nice to you.*"

4.   WHEN THE CHILD HAS LEARNED SOME GENERAL RULES
     FOR BEHAVIOR, THESE CAN NOW BE USED TO MAKE
     PLANS ABOUT ACTIONS TO BE TAKEN. The parent helps
     the child reason out a course of action or she sets limits
     before the children get out of hand.

A.   Jimmy is angry at Mickey and threatens to beat him up.
     Mother shows him that there is a rule he has learned
     which goes against this.

     MOTHER: "I can see you are angry. But what's the
               Golden Rule?"
     JIMMY: "Don't do to someone else what you
               wouldn't want him to do to you?"
     MOTHER: "That's right. Maybe we can find a better
               way to settle the issue. Hey, suppose he is
               really just trying to get you all upset. Have
               you thought of that? If you just ignored what
               he did, you would fool him if he's expecting
               you to be all upset."
     JIMMY: "Maybe. I'll give it a try. And besides, if I
               hurt him, he would just want to hurt me
               back."

B.   *A party is coming up at your house and you want to
     remind your child about showing good manners and
     going to bed on time, even though there will be a lot
     of exciting things going on.*

     MOTHER: "We're going to have company tomorrow
               night. They will be arriving about 8:30. You
               can help greet guests, but you will have to
               go to bed by 9:00. Tell me about how you
               introduce yourself and greet company."
     MARTIN: "I'd say my name is Martin . . . "
     MOTHER: "What else would you say?"
     MARTIN: "We're glad you could come?"

146

MOTHER: "That's right, you say your name and welcome them. When are you going to bed?"

MARTIN: "At 9:00."

MOTHER: "Right. Say goodnight to the company and go get ready for bed. I will come up to tuck you in."

C. *Suppose you are taking your children to the amusement park. In the past they have always gotten overexcited about all of the rides and candy and stuff, and you can't afford to have them take more than three rides and have one candy or ice cream treat. Discuss it ahead of time rather than after they are all excited.*

MOTHER: [*At the dinner table*] "After dinner your dad and I are going to take you to Kiddieland. Each of you may have three ride tickets, so be thinking about how you want to use them. We can't afford more than that. Each of you can also have one ten-cent treat, ice cream or candy or a drink. Do you understand?"

The kids are excited about going, but the rule has been set ahead of time, and they have time to prepare for what is to come. When later one of them starts to beg for "one more ride," Mother needs only to ask "How many rides did we say?"

D. *You are going to visit some friends and you want to teach your child how to be a good guest. They have a son about your son's age.*

MOTHER: "Tony, we are going to visit Mark and his mother. I want to see if you can tell me how a good guest should behave. If Mark comes to visit you what would you like him to do with your playthings?"

TONY: "I think he should ask me first if he wants to play with something."

MOTHER: "What else? Would you care if he breaks your racing car?"

TONY: "Sure. I'd send him home."

MOTHER: "Now tell me what the rule should be for you when we visit Mark."

TONY: "I should ask before I play with something."

MOTHER: "And take care of Mark's things the way he would. What should you do?"

TONY: "I should ask first, and then take good care of Mark's things."

MOTHER: "Good."

Later, be sure to note whether Tony followed the rule, and praise him if he did.

Some rules about making and using rules

Clear rules for behaving make day-to-day living easier. Children should be taught the rules for living comfortably with others— how to be helpful, cooperative, responsible, clean, healthy, and so forth. By spelling out their rules for their children, parents are in a position to know when to reinforce, when to ignore, or when to punish their children. Rules provide guides for parents in being *consistent* in training their children. Rules also help the child remember what is expected of him, since *many actions are summarized in the rule.*

MAKING RULES

1. WHERE POSSIBLE, RULES SHOULD BE SHORT, STATED POSITIVELY, AND BE EASY TO REMEMBER.

THIS WAY	NOT THIS WAY
Homework before TV.	If you don't get your homework done, you can't watch TV.
Wash hands before eating.	You can't eat unless you wash your hands.
If you get ready for bed by eight, you get a story.	If you are not in bed by eight, I won't read you a story.
If you want dessert, you must taste all foods served.	No dessert, if you don't taste everything on your plate.

2. RULES SHOULD SPECIFY A BEHAVIOR AND A CONSEQUENCE.

THIS WAY	NOT THIS WAY
You make your bed before you eat breakfast.	Make your bed each morning.
Dishes must be washed before you can watch TV.	Dishes must be washed each night.
Clean your room on Saturday before going out to play.	Clean your room each Saturday.
Taking out the trash each day by 7 p.m. earns five points (toward an allowance).	Take out the trash.
If you are on time for dinner, your food will be warm.	Be home for dinner at six o'clock.
When everyone is quiet, Father will serve dinner.	You must be quiet when you come to the dinner table.

3. RULES SHOULD BE STATED SO THAT THEY CAN BE EASILY ENFORCED.

SUB-RULES:

A. *It should be easy to know whether the rule was followed or not.*

THIS WAY	NOT THIS WAY
You must wash your hands and face, comb your hair, and be dressed in clean clothes before leaving for school.	You must look decent before leaving for school.
You must clean your room on Saturday before going out to play. By clean, I mean all toys picked up, clothes	You must clean your room on Saturday before going out to play. I want a complete job.

put away or in the hamper, vacuum the floor, dust the shelves and window ledges.

You are to set the table before dinner. That means plates, silverware, glasses, and coffee cups, salt and pepper, sugar and cream, bread and butter, napkins.

You are to set the table before dinner. Don't forget anything.

When the rule states the details of what has to be done, the child cannot make excuses for doing half of the job. You know it was done or it was not done. Vague rules are not enforceable. Be specific about what is to be done.

B. *The consequences for following the rule should be easily applied and known to be reinforcing.*

THIS WAY

NOT THIS WAY

Eat your breakfast before the school bus comes and you won't go to school hungry.

Eat your breakfast on time or you will miss the school bus. (Nick would rather miss the bus).

When you hang up your coat and hat, you can join us for dinner.

When you hang up your hat and coat, you can set the table.

For making your bed each morning, you earn three points toward your allowance.

You have to make your bed each morning before you go to school.

If you do a good job on your homework, you can make fudge with me.

If you do a good job on your homework, I'll take you fishing sometime.

If you come home on time, you'll be able to go out again another night.

If you don't come home on time, you'll have to stay in all month.

150

C. *The consequences for not following the rule should be easily applied and known to be effective.*

In all of the "This Way" examples above, failure to follow the rule leads to a loss of a reinforcer. It is also possible to enforce rules with a mild punishing consequence.

GENERAL RULE: If you make a mess, you'll have to clean it up.

SUB-RULES: If you spill your milk, get the sponge and clean it up.

If you track in mud, get the mop and clean it up.

If you write on the walls, you'll have to wash them.

GENERAL RULE: If you forget to do something, or do something wrong, you will just have to take the time to do it right before you do anything else.

SUB-RULES: If you forget to close the door, you'll have to go back and close it.

These dishes are dirty; they will have to be washed again.

Your bed is not made very neatly; try again.

4. BE SURE THE RULE IS ONE YOU CAN TEACH TO YOUR CHILD.
It is unlikely that you will teach a two-year-old to make his bed or wash the dishes. It is unlikely that you will teach a child to wash his hands before he eats if there is no water readily available. Rules must be reasonable and suitable to the child's age, abilities, and the living conditions.

USING RULES

1. START NEW RULES ONE AT A TIME.
Get one rule going before starting a new one.

2. WHEN A RULE IS BROKEN, ASK THE CHILD TO STATE THE RULE HE BROKE AS PART OF THE CORRECTION. Many times, just reminding the child what the rule is can stop the *undesired behavior.*

EXAMPLE: *Ernie starts out to play before emptying the trash.*

> MOTHER: "What's the rule, Ernie?"
>
> ERNIE: "We finish our chores before going out to play."
>
> MOTHER: "That's right."

Ernie finishes his chore and nothing else need be said.

3. WHEN A RULE IS BROKEN, HAVE THE CORRECT BEHAVIOR PERFORMED BEFORE THE CHILD DOES ANYTHING ELSE, IF IT IS POSSIBLE. It is not possible to have a child undo coming home late. A child can't un-spill his milk. A child cannot un-hit someone. But a child can be asked to go back and close the door, put away his shoes, do the forgotten dishes, take out the forgotten trash, or say the forgotten "Thank you."

4. USE REMINDERS TO TEACH RULES AND THEN FADE THEM OUT. Reminders might consist of signs, notes, charts, check lists, or words spoken before the task is to be undertaken.

A CHECK LIST ON DISHES MIGHT SAY:

1. Fill sink with water.
2. Add two capfuls of detergent.
3. Wash dishes, then cups and glasses, then silverware, then pots and pans.
4. Dry them and put them away.
5. Wash counter.
6. Clean sink.
7. Put away detergent, towels, and dishpan.

A chart might look like the one we made for Teresa in Unit 4. The chart helps Teresa remember how to earn points by completing a number of tasks.

As the notes or charts are no longer needed, since good habits have been formed, they can be removed in steps. The checklist becomes a sign "Do Dishes." Teresa's chart is taken away, but her mother keeps track and still bases an allowance on her performance that week. Reminders should be *faded out* slowly, not taken away all at once.

5. IGNORE PROTESTS ABOUT RULES.
Do not get trapped into arguing with your child about the "fairness" or "reasonableness" of a rule. Do not get trapped into making one exception after another. Behave with the attitude "That's the way it is." Stay cool, calm, and collected. Get involved in other activities if necessary to keep from attending to the refusal to do it, or verbal protest. Take the attitude that the job is going to be done, the rule followed, if we do nothing else all day. You can last longer than your child.

Protests are likely at first when you change from one approach to another. Expect such protests, but be prepared to wait them out. They will go away if you do not reinforce them by "giving in," "giving lots of attention to them" or "arguing with your child about them."

Following instructions

Most parents want their children to do what they are asked to do without a lot of fuss and bother. However, parents also do not want a fearful child who will follow any kind of authority figure. It is possible to have a well-behaved child without having a fearful child by following two rules:
1. Use positive consequences to teach your child to do what you ask him to do. Minimize the use of threats and punishment.
2. Do not ask a child to do something unless you really want him to do it. Be prepared to insist on it by waiting with him until it is done.

To teach a child to follow instructions, you start by asking him to do things you know he can do and even likes to do. You then praise him or reward him in other ways for doing as he was asked.

The next step is to ask him to do more difficult things or things which are more like work. Slowly increase the task effort required, but continue to reinforce success.

Finally, make reinforcement intermittent and unpredictable.

Teaching this task is just a special case of teaching a child to follow rules. There is really nothing new about it. We have simply taught the child to follow the general rule:

DO WHAT I ASK YOU TO DO
AND I WILL REWARD YOU.

Summary

The complete rule about "what is learned" says: The child learns to do under a given set of conditions what is reinforced. Reasons, rules, and reminders help the child learn when to do what, or when not to do something. Reasons, rules, and reminders also help the child learn to manage his own behavior.

Teaching a child to reason about his behavior is accomplished in steps:
1. *At first you simply tell your child what he did to earn a reward or punishment.*
2. *Next, you begin to ask him to state the reasons for reinforcement or punishment.*
3. *When your child can state reasons for specific behaviors, tie these into more general rules about behavior.*
4. *When general rules for behavior have been taught, these can be used to plan about actions to come.*

Rules not only provide guides in helping children remember what is expected of them; they also help the parents be consistent in training their children.

MAKING RULES
1. *Where possible (and it is not always possible or desirable), rules should be short, stated positively, and be easy to remember.*
2. *Rules should specify a behavior and a consequence.*

3. *Rules should be stated so that they can be easily enforced.*
   A. *It should be easy to know whether the rule was followed or not.*
   B. *The consequences for following the rule should be easily applied and known to be reinforcing.*
   C. *The consequences for not following the rule should be easily applied and known to be effective.*
4. *Be sure the rule is one you can teach your child.*

USING RULES
1. *Start new rules out one at a time.*
2. *When a rule is broken, ask the child to state the rule he broke.*
3. *When a rule is broken, have the correct behavior performed if possible.*
4. *Use reminders to teach rules and then fade them out.*
5. *Ignore protests about rules as long as you are sure they are reasonable.*

Teaching a child to follow instructions (obedience) is the same as teaching the rule "Do what I ask you to do."

Unit 9 • Exercise 1

Place one word in each blank or follow the other instructions given.

1. Mrs. E. was instructed to make her ——————————— clear.

2. The following is an example of Grandma's Rule: "You can go out and play, ——————————— you finish your chores."

3. Mrs. James found that giving out tickets helped ——————————— or cue herself to use praise.

4. In escaping the criticism trap, we suggested putting up signs to help ——————————— you to praise.

5. We have to teach a child not only what to do, but ——————————— to do it.

6. The complete rule about "what is learned" says: The child learns to do *under a given set of* ——————————— what is reinforced.

7. A ——————————— light tells us when not to cross the street.

8. A green light tells us ——————————— to cross the street.

9. When a child is taught rules about ——————————— of his behaviors, he can make better decisions for himself when his parents are not there.

10. A child can be taught to follow the rule "First we work and then we _____.

11. The first step in teaching a child to "reason out" the consequences of behavior is to _____ your child what he did to earn a reward or punishment.

12. After a child has been given many examples of reasons for reinforcement or reasons for punishment, begin to ask _____ to state the reasons.

13. When your child answers your question, say the _____ thing back to him. "Yes, you've earned a special treat _____ you did such a good job of cleaning your room."

14. When your child can state reasons for specific behaviors, begin to work on _____ _____ for behavior.

15. General rules are taught by showing how a specific behavior and consequence is an _____ of a more general rule. For example, "You did the dishes on time, so you will get to see your TV program. When you do your chores, good things happen."

16. When general rules for behavior have been taught, these can be used to make _____ about actions to come. The parent helps the child reason out a course of action or she sets limits _____ the children get out of hand.

17. Jimmy's mother used the Golden Rule to help him decide that _____ Mickey was not the best thing to do.

18. Martin's mother reminded him ahead of time about showing _____ _____ and going to _____ on time even though a party was going on.

19. When a rule is established before children get overly involved in exciting things, it is _____ likely that the rule will be followed.

20. Mother helped Tony be a _____ _____ by reasoning with him about the behavior he would expect of guests in his house.

21. Rules should be short, stated positively, and be easy to _____.

22. Rules should specify a behavior and a _____.

23. Rules should be stated so that they can be easily _____.

24. Be sure any rule you make is one you can _____ to your child.

CIRCLE ONE

25. The following rule is stated positively: "If you are not in bed by eight, I won't read you a story."   yes   no

26. The following is an example of a short rule: "Homework before TV."   yes   no

27. The following is an example of a positive rule: "Wash your hands before eating."   yes   no

28. The following rule specifies a consequence: "Clean your room each Saturday!"   yes   no

29. The following rule specifies a consequence: "When everyone is quiet, Father will serve dinner."   yes   no

30. The following rule is easy to enforce: "You must look decent before leaving for school."   yes   no

31. The following rule is easy to enforce: "You have to make your bed each morning before going to school."   yes   no

32. The following rule is easy to enforce: "If you make a mess, you'll have to clean it up."   yes   no

33. A rule can be called reasonable if it can be easily _____ to your child.

34. In using rules we should teach only _____ rule at a time.

35. If a rule is broken, a good practice is to ask the child to _____ _____ _____ he broke.

36. When a rule is broken, have the child perform the _____ behavior when that is possible.

37. Use reminders to teach new rules and then _____ them out.

38. Ignore _____ about rules, as long as you are sure they are reasonable.

Unit 9 • Exercise 2

PRACTICE IN WRITING RULES

A. Rewrite the following rules so that they are stated positively:

1. You can't come to breakfast until your bed is made.

_____

_____

2. If you are late for dinner, your food will be cold.

_____

_____

3. You can't go to movie unless you finish your chores.

_____

_____

4. If you come home late from school, you can't go out and play after dinner.

_____

_____

B. Specify a consequence appropriate for each of the following:

1. Going to bed on time.

_____

2. Not getting out of bed after being put to bed.

_____

3. Playing cooperatively with brother.

_____

4. Cleaning the garage.

    _____

5. Mowing the lawn.

    _____

C. Rewrite these rules to make them enforceable:

1. No fighting going to or from school or you lose your
    allowance.

    _____

    _____

2. Do the dishes before 7 p.m.

    _____

    _____

Unit 9 • Exercise 3

WEAKENING AN UNDESIRED BEHAVIOR

1. Select a behavior from the group you observed last week, Unit 8, Exercise 3. Define the behavior here:

   _____

   _____

2. You may use any method presented so far in this program to change your target behavior. Record your method here:

   _____

   _____

   _____

   _____

3. On the next page, record notes for the next two weeks on the success of your approach. If no progress is made in one week, change your method for the second week. My new method is:

   _____

   _____

   _____

   _____

   _____

   _____

TARGET BEHAVIOR _____

DAY	HOW OFTEN DID IT OCCUR TODAY?	COMMENTS
1.		
2.		
3.		
4.		
5.		
6.		
7.		
8.		
9.		
10.		
11.		
12.		
13.		
14.		

Unit 10
YOUR CHILD'S PERSONALITY AND YOU

The ways in which children have been taught to respond to other people are called social behaviors. Usually, when we talk about a child's *personality* we are talking about his social behaviors which occur frequently. A child who seeks much attention, praise, or help from adults is said to be dependent. A child who frequently hits, pushes, or takes things away from another child is said to be aggressive. A child who smiles frequently, talks freely to others, and spends a lot of time with other people is called sociable. The child who spends little time with people is called withdrawn or fearful.

Parents have often thought or been told that their child's *personality* came with the baby. We now know that how parents and others teach a child to behave is very important. In this final unit we will look at some of the ways in which a child's social behavior is built or changed.

Dependent children

"I CAN'T DO IT. HELP ME."

Babies are not able to do some things for themselves. Parents dress them, feed them, and care for their needs. When the parent continues to do things for a child beyond the point where the child could be taught to do these things for himself, the child is reinforced for not growing up (or learning more adult behaviors). Very likely such behaviors are intermittently reinforced, since parents are not always able to help in a busy household.

This problem can be avoided if from the start the mother encourages (reinforces) the child's efforts to do things for himself. The key to success is not to expect too much too soon. Reinforce *trying* at first, then small steps of progress.

In older children this problem can take the form of not knowing what to play or not being able to make decisions. The parent needs to train the child to do things for himself, to choose play activities for himself, to make decisions. This is done by reinforcing steps of progress, giving suggestions and reminders only to the extent needed, and slowly fading out the parent's help.

Karen, age six, would not get up, dress herself, and eat her breakfast on time for school unless her mother was nagging or helping every step of the way. Mother reinforced her "help me" behaviors in part because she thought that was what mothers were for, and in part because she was afraid Karen would be late for school.

Since the tasks were those Karen could do, the problem was handled by getting Karen an alarm clock, telling her she was responsible for getting ready for school, stopping all nagging, and praising her for her successes.

Karen's teacher was informed about what was being done and asked not to give her extra attention if she came late. Mother kept records of her progress.

Karen was late for school six times in the first two weeks, but only once in the second two weeks. In the next six weeks, Karen left home a little late about once a week, but hurried to school on time. Mother was pleased with the change in relationships. "This is now her problem, not mine. The whole situation is very much improved." Karen was very proud of herself on the days she left for school early and received praise for this.

At seven, Linda was still insisting that one of her parents cut her meat for her. Her parents had never given her training in how to hold a knife and fork to cut meat. For a long time it was easier at dinner time just to do it for her. After a long period of criticizing her for not cutting her meat, followed by doing it for her, they took time to show her how to cut meat. This was done several times and Linda was praised for her success. For awhile, Linda continued to ask to have her meat cut, but this was ignored or she was quietly told to work on it herself. Training quickly removed this problem.

Larry grunted instead of asking for things, particularly at the dinner table. His older brother would usually guess what he wanted and speak for him. Larry did not have to talk and got quite a bit of attention for his cute gestures. The problem was handled by reminding Larry at first what he should say, "Say, 'please pass the milk,'" and not giving him the milk until he asked for it. Later the reminders were withheld and the parents pretended not to understand the grunts. Only spoken requests were reinforced by responding to them.

EMOTIONAL OUTBURSTS RELATED TO A CHANGE IN REINFORCEMENT

When reinforcement for any behavior is withdrawn, we are initially upset. A mother who no longer reinforces "help me" behaviors will find this to be so also. Parents should be prepared to take some outbursts without "giving in" to quiet the child, or without getting angry. *Ignore* the irrelevant emotional behaviors. They will drop out in a short time. The first few outbursts are usually the longest. Stay with your change program and you will succeed.

"HOLD ME"

The "hold me" child is most likely to be a toddler, because after awhile he gets too heavy to hold and his mother quits reinforcing holding. However, clingy children can be found at all ages, children who want to stay near Mommy and constantly seek comforting. Such children are sometimes called fearful and insecure, but this is not necessarily so. Such behavior can be a problem when it occurs very often, since it is incompatible with a child learning many social skills..

AN ADULT-ORIENTED CHILD, ANN[1]

Ann was four. She was from an upper middle class family. Ann reacted freely with adults but did not play with children. She was not withdrawn or frightened. As time went on she spent more and more time just standing and looking. Often she retired to a make-believe bed in the play yard to "sleep" for a few minutes. Less than fifteen per cent of her time was spent playing with peers. About forty per cent of the time she was interacting with adults.

A program was devised to encourage more peer interaction. When Ann was alone, she was given no attention from the teachers. If she came to the teacher with another child, attention was given. Coming to teacher alone was given minimal attention. When Ann was playing with another child, teacher would go to them and give attention and play materials. For example, "You three girls have a cozy house. Here are some more cups, Ann, for your tea party." If Ann began to leave the group while teacher was there, the teacher turned away from her and attended to other children. During the six weeks of this program, Ann's play with children quickly increased to about sixty per cent of the time, and interactions with adults dropped to under twenty per cent. Isolate play dropped from about forty-five per cent to twenty per cent of the time. Attention from adults was slowly faded out and the peer play continued on its own.

Clinging behavior can be changed if you recognize one important point. The clingy child is *reinforced by social reinforcers* (attention, affection, praise) *from adults*. Thus, these *same reinforcers* can be used to strengthen independent behaviors such as playing alone, exploring the house and yard, learning motor skills, or playing with other children. Mother *suggests* a small step out toward some interesting activity, gives support as needed to steps away from her, and gets busy with "other things" if her child just clings. Praise is given for being a "big boy" or "big girl." "I saw you swinging all by yourself. That's really a big boy." As the fun of doing other things becomes the reinforcer for the child's behavior, the mother has to suggest less and reinforce less.

CRY BABIES

One of the neatest demonstrations of the effects of reinforcement we have ever seen was made by Etzel and Gerwitz. The nurses in the hospital nursery had been picking up a week-old child when he cried and had made a cry baby out of him. Etzel and Gerwitz showed that they could make him into a smiling baby by ignoring crying and reinforcing smiling.

It is understandable how high rates of crying get started. Mothers worry about their young ones being in pain and can't always tell what is wrong. Also after a few months, her going to the baby and picking him up is often enough to quiet him. *This reinforces mother for picking baby up* because the irritating crying stops. It's like the criticism trap. The very behavior a mother wants to reduce (crying) is increased by her actions. The more baby is picked up after he cries, the more he will cry. As a general rule, if the mother is assured that there is nothing physically wrong with her infant, it is best that she pick him up when he is not crying. A child in pain, however, shouldn't be neglected.

LITTLE HURTS

Excessive crying from the toddler is usually tied to the little bumps and bruises that come with learning to walk and run. If a mother is overly responsive to the hurt child, she can teach her child to scream and yell at the smallest upset. The problem is avoided by giving real hurts the attention and comfort needed, but being more matter-of-fact about the minor bumps and bruises.

Excessive crying in the older child is handled just as for younger children, only it might take more persistence on mother's part before a change is produced. Be sure your child is all right with a brief, casual check. Then get busy with "other things" to get your attention away from the crying child. Give attention and praise for not crying and for being a "big boy."

MISBEHAVING TO GET ATTENTION

Children like Peter (Unit 1) whose misbehavior was reinforced by attention from mother are also sometimes called dependent. As long as we know what causes the behavior (attention from adults), it doesn't matter what we call it. Misbehaving to get attention can also be caused by attention from other children. The following case was reported by Dorothy Kirk.

Susan is ten, outgoing, and normal. She has an older and a younger sister, as well as a brother, Robert, who is twelve. Recently, Robert started to tease Susan in the pre-dinner hour, while Mother was fixing dinner. The teasing was such that Mother could not put her finger on anything explicit to deal with. Robert would just stand by Susan and look at what she was doing until she noticed him. Sometimes he took a book which he knew Susan usually looked at and would claim to have it first. Sometimes he would take a little too much time to get out of Susan's way or to hand something back to her.

Susan would react to all this by screaming and verbally attacking Robert. She would run to her mother to protest. Mother tried telling both of them to cut it out, but it did no good. "Robert wasn't doing anything," although every move was calculated to tease Susan. Robert even suggested to his mother that he probably wouldn't do it if Susan didn't react so strongly. Before long Susan was running to Mother every few minutes to complain.

The change procedure consisted of Mother ignoring Susan's coming to her to complain. Mother simply said, "I'm sorry, it's your problem. You will have to solve it yourself." Praise was to be given Susan for not complaining.

On the first day, Susan ran to her mother eight times in one hour. Mother said it was her problem to solve.

On the second day, she again came to her mother eight times, and her screams were louder. Mother ignored.

On the third day, Susan sought constant attention from her mother and was verbally abusive to Mother. Mother ignored and repeated her statement, "It's your problem."

On the fourth day, Susan again came in eight times, but gave up quickly when her mother ignored her.

On the fifth day, Susan appealed to her mother only four times. She was overly polite and did not scream. She had also tried "controlled politeness" with Robert without success. Susan still wanted her mother to punish Robert. Mother said, "I'm sorry, I won't."

On the sixth day, Susan made one bid for attention at the beginning of the hour. She accused her mother of not loving her and said she was going to run away. Susan put on warm clothes and left the house. The rest had dinner. Susan's older sister helped Mother keep track of Susan without Mother giving attention. Susan didn't leave the yard. Mother finally went out to find Susan by a tree in the back yard. She was feeling sorry for herself. They had a talk. Mother praised her for finding some other solution than complaining to Mother, but her mother was not sure running away was the best th'ng to do. Mother suggested that Susan learn to ignore Robert's teasing completely. She said it worked for her when Mother's older brother used to tease her. Susan didn't think it would work.

The next day Susan intentionally ignored Robert. Robert got less subtle in his teasing, and Susan just got up and left the room. Susan was praised by her mother. The following evening, Susan continued to ignore Robert and he quit teasing after a couple tries. A little later Susan asked Robert to play a game with her. He smiled and accepted. Mother was pleased and let them know it.

There were only two minor incidents in the next six weeks. In both cases Susan did not come to her mother. After an initial criticism, she invited Robert to join her in play.

A PASSIVE BOY

The inactive or "passive" boy is usually not fun for other boys to play with and is likely to be excluded from play groups. *Mark was such an inactive boy* in an experimental nursery school.[2] He showed little interaction with his peers.

The teachers decided to reinforce climbing activity to see what effect this might have on peer relations. Climbing on the jungle gym was the target behavior. Before the program was begun, frequency of climbing on anything was less than five per cent of the time spent outside. Social reinforcement was then given Mark anytime he climbed on the jungle gym. By the end of nine days, Mark spent over sixty per cent of his time outside climbing His peer interactions changed. He became a happy and active member of several boys' play groups. Mark also talked more with peers. Active boys play with active boys.

BEDTIME CRYING

This is easily avoided from the start by following a consistent bedtime routine and matter–of–factly putting your child to bed and leaving him. If he cries on being left, this is ignored. The young child will quickly learn not to cry at bedtime.

Problems are most apt to arise when parents are in the habit of rocking or walking an infant until he is asleep. When later they decide that this is too much work, the child cries fretfully. Several nights of long crying may be needed to build a new sleep pattern.

Bedtime crying can also be taught if repeated getting up is reinforced by a drink, a treat, or extra attention, and then the parents decide to stop that. Again, a new routine can be estab lished if you are careful to be consistent about enforcing the new rule. "You must stay in your bed after I say good night." Crying is ignored and the door is closed if he breaks the rule (or he is matter–of–factly returned to bed as many times as necessary). It should not take more than a week to build a more satisfactory bedtime routine.

SEPARATION CRYING

If mother is a strong learned reinforcer for her child, her leaving can be a withdrawal of reinforcement and, therefore, produce some emotional upset. This emotional behavior will become intense under two conditions: (1) if the child is not properly cared for in mother's absence; or (2) mother starts to leave, but gives in when the child cries and stays. Condition 2 reinforces emotional outbursts. As long as your child is properly cared for in your absence, and as long as you do not reinforce the minor upset which goes with first separations, you will have no problem. Your child will settle down within minutes after you leave.

A program to get rid of long and intense crying on mother's leaving

1. Be sure the child is first familiar with the sitter and has had fun with this sitter with Mommy present. (The sitter could be father.)
2. Mother should leave with a simple hug and "goodbye," and if the child is old enough, with words about when she will be back.
3. If the child fusses and cries, the sitter should pay no attention to the child until he stops crying. Then a fun activity should be started. A special treat might be planned.
4. At first Mother should plan to be away for short periods, then gradually increase the time away. In any case, she should not return while her child is still crying.
5. Leaving the child with different people is the final step.

Aggressive children

For the most part, children are taught to be aggressive. Some forms of aggression are reinforced by society at large, such as competitive sports, soldiering, or the behavior of a policeman doing his job. Most boys are taught to defend themselves. Many boys are trained to box, tackle, duel, or use guns. Vigorous responses are important to success in many activities.

The rules about aggression a child must learn in our culture are complex. The toddler is reinforced for pushing harder on a stuck door, but not for pushing baby down in the playpen. The three-year-old is reinforced for throwing the ball to Daddy, but not through a window. Jill is not punished if knocking Jeff down has a reasonable explanation, but is punished if it was intentional. Jimmy is praised for defending himself against an older bully, but not for hitting Janice. In the area of intense responses, the child has a hard time learning the rules about just when you do what. In addition, the parent's task in teaching children is not an easy one. In this section we will look at some common behaviors usually called aggressive and see what to do about them.

THROWING TANTRUMS
In response to seemingly minor events some children will flop on the floor and pound their arms, legs, or heads, and scream and

yell. Some will attack their parent, and others will hold their breath until they turn blue or even pass out. Temper tantrums have their beginning in the minor emotional upsets which go with the loss of reinforcers. Suppose a child is used to eating various snacks before dinner, and Mother decides to stop this. She says, "No, you must wait for dinner." Joe stamps his feet and cries that he's hungry and his mother gives in. Imagine the process taking place many times. Mother tries to wait Joe out, but he comes on even stronger. Mother gives in again. Slowly Joe is reinforced for more intense protest behavior. Intense forms of protest are labeled tantrums. They are behaviors which have been taught through withholding reinforcers and then giving in and giving the withheld reinforcers.

The parent who follows the guidelines for training set forth in this manual is not likely to run into tantrums. If they already exist, however, you need a way to get rid of them. Even severe tantrums can be eliminated in as little as three or four days. The procedure is nearly the same as that used for excessive crying. The child is left alone until he is quiet for several minutes. He may be placed in a room by himself, or he can be in the same room with the parent if the parent is good at ignoring. The first time a parent tries to ignore a tantrum to get rid of it, the tantrum can last an hour or more. By the third or fourth trial, it should last less than a minute or two.

If an isolation room is used, remove possible dangers. Be prepared for possible broken windows and have a way of checking on the safety of your child without giving him attention. The room should be lighted, but with playthings removed. Tell your child just what will happen if he tantrums. Tell him he will have to stay there until he is quiet and is ready to join the family again. When the tantrum occurs, be matter–of–fact in placing him in the room. Carry him in if necessary. Return him or lock the door if he comes out. You must be more persistent in your goals than he, or you will end up simply strengthening his tantrums. The intense yelling of a child is upsetting to a parent, but keep in mind your goals. With consistent handling, the problem is readily stopped and the basis for a better interaction with parents formed.

NEGATIVISM — "I DON'T WANT TO."

"I won't do it." "No." "I don't want to." Protest behaviors generally get started because children are not being managed in a positive way. They continue, once they are started, because they pay off; that is, parents "reason" or "argue" or otherwise give attention to the protests, and now and then let the children have their way.

Negativism can be avoided for the most part by following the ideas presented in Units 7 and 8 on how to reinforce and punish. If the child is intently involved in some activity, do not insist that he suddenly leave it. Give him a warning so that he has time to bring the activity to a planned end. Make the new behavior you want him to undertake as attractive as possible. Say, "It's time for your bedtime story," rather than, "Stop whatever you are doing and get ready for bed." Or, "Will you do me a favor and get the paper for me?" — instead of giving a command. Make the new activity fun. One can also avoid negative reactions by giving the child a choice of two alternatives:

1. "Would you rather finish what you are doing and not have your story tonight, or come now and have your story?"
2. "You can either take turns and not fight, or you will have to play by yourselves."

Often we provoke negative reactions by being too abrupt, too bossy, and too negative ourselves. If strong negativism has already developed, look to see how much attention it is given by you. Do not get trapped into acting insulted by a disobedient, disrespectful child. Begin to use some of the suggestions given above for making interactions more positive, and consider other ways of increasing the reinforcement given to your child for good behavior.

THE BOSSY CHILD
Bossy children very likely learned to give orders by observing their parents. Also, bossing often does lead others to do what you want. It works often enough to become a strong and persistent behavior.

A common mild form of bossy behavior is observed at the dinner table. A child says "gimme" rather than "please pass the milk." Dinner time provides a good chance to train polite social behavior. If mother does not pass the food when asked for it in a bossy way, the child will soon learn to ask politely. Reminders may have to be given at first. "Say, 'please.'" It also helps to place all the food by father and have him serve it, rather than leaving the food where it can be reached. Father then serves each child less than he will eat so that they will have to ask for more. Father then hears only polite requests. There are other benefits to this procedure. The children have to wait while others are being served. Since waiting is followed by eating, patience is being taught. The order in which the children are served can be used as a reward also.

The general rules are: Do not be bossy yourself, and do not reinforce bossy orders from your child.

FIGHTING — HITTING, KICKING, AND BITING OTHERS.

All children learn to hit, kick, and bite. You can hit a baseball, kick a football, and bite a steak, but we don't usually want children to use these responses to hurt people. Training a child not to make responses which hurt other people is done more easily with two- and three-year-olds than later. Often a mild scolding, restraint, or a "don't" are all that is needed at this age. A quick bite back is sometimes useful in teaching the young child that biting does hurt. Many suggestions have been provided throughout this book for dealing with fighting. Let us just summarize them here:

1. Be sure the hitting and kicking no longer pays off.
2. Use punishment by withdrawal of reinforcers so as not to provide an aggressive model.
3. Reinforce cooperative behaviors.
4. Use rules and reminders to help get the new behavior going.
5. Look ahead to possible trouble and prepare your child for it.

VERBAL ABUSE

Name calling and swearing can be learned through modeling parents or peers. The behavior is probably reinforced by the "upsetting effects" it has on others and by the attention it receives. Quite often children will say "I hate you," or "You are a nasty momma" to their mothers. If a parent over-reacts to such comments by being hurt or trying to find out what's wrong, the child may well learn to use such comments to get you to be more attentive.

In general, the first and best approach to verbal aggression is to ignore it. Act like it did not happen. Give attention only to acceptable verbal behavior. "Sticks and stones will break my bones but names will never hurt me." Names don't hurt. One can use ignoring to weaken their use.

For some verbal aggression reinforced by peers, this may not be enough. A *response cost** system might be tried. It goes

---

response cost: Each wrong response costs the child the loss of a point, token, or other reinforcer.

like this. The child decides on a gift to work toward. When he has earned two hundred points, he can get the gift. Each day he is given ten or fifteen points. Each time the parents hear the child swear or use other verbal aggression, they say, "That'll cost you a point." A record is kept of points earned each day, which is also a record of progress in reducing swearing. Such a system could be tied to an allowance, or the payoff could be an activity reinforcer the child has selected. Bonus points might be given for times when the child was in a difficult situation and did not cuss or swear.

JEALOUSY
The arrival of a new child typically results in sets of conditions where there is a loss of reinforcement for the older children. Mother is gone for a period, attention is being given more to the new one, and so forth. Some of the emotional reactions which go with the loss of reinforcement can occur. In this case we call them jealousy. Such reactions can be prevented by preparing against them. Be sure there is adequate care of the older children when mother is gone. Allow them to talk to her by phone. Father should give extra attention to them. When the new baby comes the dangers lie in the attention and gifts usually showered on the baby. Have your friends give attention to the older children, too. Let the older child be responsible for opening the gifts. Take time to teach the older child to be helpful in caring for the new one.

When an older child acts more like a baby after a new baby comes, this has been interpreted as due to jealousy. The behaviors of wanting a bottle or crawling again are called "regressive." Actually the older child simply sees the behavior of the baby reinforced and would like some reinforcement, too. So he behaves like the baby. There is little harm as long as too much attention is not given to it. If the older child wants a bottle, let him try it. He won't want it for long. It's too slow a way to get milk. The parent should focus on reinforcing "big boy" and "big girl" behaviors — being helpful, strong, and skillful.

Summary

In the final unit we have looked at some of the more common social behavior problems children have and what you can do to avoid or eliminate such problems. For the most part your child will learn to be the kind of person you teach him to be. You can teach him to be aggressive or dependent in many different ways.

- **WE BUILD THE SOCIAL ENVIRONMENT WHICH CONTROLS US BY THE WAY WE REINFORCE AND PUNISH EACH OTHER.**

- **PEOPLE TEACH EACH OTHER HOW TO BEHAVE.**

- **BE A GOOD TEACHER.**

NOTES TO UNIT 10

[1] K.E. Allen, B. Hart, J.S. Buel, F.R. Harris, and M.M. Wolf, "Effects of Social Reinforcement on Isolate Behavior of a Nursery School Child," *Child Development,* XXXV (1964), 511-518.

[2] Margaret K. Johnston, C. Susan Kelley, Florence R. Harris, and Montrose M. Wolf, "An Application of Reinforcement Principles to Development of Motor Skills of a Young Child," *Child Development,* XXXVII (June, 1966), 380-387.

Unit 10 • Exercise 1

For each of the social behavior problems indicated, write a few notes as to how you might correct the problem.

1. Jimmy at age six cannot tie his shoes. He comes repeatedly to Mommy and says, "Help me."

    _____

    _____

    _____

    _____

2. Aaron, age five, seems afraid to play with the boys. He always wants to be by Mommy. He seldom leaves the yard or has friends over.

    _____

    _____

    _____

    _____

3. Margie, age eight, cries long and loud at the slightest little hurt.

    _____

    _____

    _____

    _____

4. Debra, age nine, throws a tantrum whenever her mother crosses her. Mother usually sends the other children to another room and stays with Debra by herself.

_____

_____

_____

_____

5. Billy, age five, cries whenever his mother leaves him.

_____

_____

_____

_____

6. Timmy keeps teasing Rolanda by watching everything she does, and making snide little picky comments. Rolanda usually gets mad and goes to her mother.

_____

_____

_____

_____

7. Billy constantly protests, "I don't want to." Mother tries to "reason" with him about why he should do what she wants him to do. It takes quite a bit of her time.

_____

_____

_____

_____

8. Linda keeps ordering her younger brother around. He doesn't like it and complains to his mother. Mother tells Linda to leave him alone, but it doesn't help.

_____

_____

_____

_____

9. Raymond fights with brother Edsel nearly every day. They are a year and a half apart in age, six and seven and a half. They never really hurt each other badly but their complaints to Mother are annoying to her.

_____

_____

_____

_____

10. Terry's mother is going to have a baby. What might you have her think about doing to keep Terry from getting jealous?

_____

_____

_____

_____

Be sure to continue your Behavior Change Project from Unit 9, Exercise 3.

EVALUATION OF PROGRESS FOR PARENTS

CITY_____ **STATE**_____

1. What did you learn from this program of value to you and your family?

   _____

   _____

   _____

   _____

2. Which exercises did you like best?

   _____

   _____

3. Which units were the most helpful?

   _____

   _____

4. Which units were the most interesting?

   _____

   _____

5. How can the program be improved?

   _____

   _____

   _____

6. Which units were the least helpful? Why?

_____

_____

_____

7. Which exercises were the least helpful? Why?

_____

_____

_____

8. Which units were dull or too difficult? Say why if you can.

_____

_____

_____

Send to: RESEARCH PRESS COMPANY
2612 North Mattis Avenue
Champaign, Illinois 61820

Answers to Questions

Unit 1 • Exercise 1

1. environment
2. rule
3. consequences
4. incompatible
5. reinforcers
6. weaken
7. control
8. punishment (or pain)
9. environment (s)
10. controls
11. happier
12. environment
    teaching
13. damaged (or injured)
14. toys
    food
15. punish
16. tantrum
17. reinforce
18. desirable (or good)
19. warn
    physical affection (or physical attention)
20. objectionable (bad)
21. first
22. quiet (order, control)
23. shouting
24. short
25. 50-90 (any number between these)
26. active
27. behavior
28. rules
29. ignored
30. praised
31. good
32. ignore
33. rules
34. strengthen (increase)
35. punishers
36. reinforcers
37. reinforcer
38. reinforcing
39. reinforcers
40. strengthen
41. punishing
42. punishment
43. reinforcing

Unit 2 • Exercises 1 & 2

1.	weaken	1.	S
2.	training (learning)	2.	A
3.	unlearned (unconditioned)	3.	T
4.	punishers	4.	U
5.	following	5.	A
6.	reinforcers (good things)	6.	S
7.	punisher	7.	U
8.	reinforcers (rewards)	8.	T
9.	traded (exchanged)	9.	A
10.	behavior	10.	S
11.	social	11.	U
12.	things	12.	T
13.	token	13.	U
14.	things	14.	A
	traded (exchanged, turned in)	15.	T
15.	is not	16.	S
16.	is	17.	S
17.	before	18.	S
18.	watching	19.	A
19.	reinforcer (reward)	20.	U
	not	21.	A
20.	less	22.	S
21.	social	23.	U
22.	behavior	24.	A
23.	c	25.	A
24.	d	26.	S
25.	social	27.	S
26.	reinforcers (rewards)	28.	S
27.	token reinforcers	29.	A
28.	social reinforcers	30.	U
29.	behavior (response)	31.	A
30.	watch (observe, count, etc.)	32.	U
	reinforcing (preferred)	33.	S
31.	reinforcer (reward, payoff)		
32.	contingent		

Unit 2 • Exercise 3

This exercise will be used for group discussion during the next session. No answers are provided here.

Unit 3 • Exercise 1

1. immediately (right now)
2. delay
3. delayed
4. reinforce
5. more (several)
6. some (a few)
7. not
8. nag
9. dawdle (delay)
10. dressed
11. attention
12. wrong
13. talking
14. often
15. praised
16. reinforce (reward, attend to)
17. attention
18. telling
19. any (all)
20. social
21. every (all the)
22. intermittently (now and then)
23. faster
24. persistent
25. unpredictable
26. intermittent
27. unpredictable
28. present (there)
29. unpredictable
30. longer
31. points
32. ice cream bar
33. points
    praise (reward)
34. improvement (getting better)
35. better
36. rewards (reinforcement)
37. trying
38. bad habits (undesirable behaviors)
39. consistent

Unit 3 • Exercise 2

This exercise will be used for group discussion during the next session. No answers are provided here.

Unit 4 • Exercise 1

1. off
2. punishing
3. criticism
   reinforcers
4. emotionally
5. reward (reinforcement)
6. points
   school
7. note
   points
8. money
9. 50
   61
10. positive (good)
11. failure
12. drop out
13. immediate
14. success
15. stronger
16. easily
17. reinforcer (reward)
18. learned
19. lot
    less
20. paired
21. reinforcing
22. reinforcing
23. marks
24. quickly (readily)
    easily
25. variety

26. increased (raised)
    less
27. token
28. traded (exchanged)
29. variety (lot)
30. praise (social
    reinforcement)
31. notes
    watch television
32. hurt
    check marks
33. 10
34. carpentry tools
35. cooperatively (nicely)
36. tickets
37. 5 - 10
38. praised
39. spending money
40. praise
    scolding (criticizing)
41. checks (marks)
42. will not (does not)
43. not doing
44. do (learn)
45. change
    effective (stronger)

Unit 4 • Exercise 2

This exercise will be used for group discussion during the next session. No answers are provided here.

Unit 5 • Exercise 1

1. strengthened (reinforced)
2. punished
3. punished
   attention
4. followed (rewarded)
5. reinforced
6. consequence (reinforcer)
   faster (sooner, more quickly)
7. reinforcing (rewarding)
8. asking for help
9. reinforced (rewarded)
10. punished
    punisher
11. contingent
12. bargaining power (reinforcers)
13. inconsiderate
14. way
15. control
16. punishment (pain)
17. environment
18. controls
19. happier
20. environment
    teaching
21. punishment
22. reinforce
23. reinforce
24. ready for bed
25. Tom or Reggie

Unit 5 • Exercise 2

1. alarm noise stopped
2. feet got cold
3. pain
4. (to bath) not punished
5. saw herself (did not like it)
6. cold water
7. cold stopped
8. warm water
9. warm, soothing water
10. ate it
11. Mommy put on shoes and socks
12. car started
13. a hug and kiss
14. no ticket
15. took a sip
16. "yes"
17. paycheck
18. getting a raise
19. Marge hugged back
20. talked to Tom

Unit 6 • Exercise 1

1. stood up
2. reinforcer
3. signal (cue)
4. works
5. opposite
6. criticism
7. reinforced
   stop
8. increased
9. attention
10. attending
    rewarding (praising, reinforcing)
11. better
12. criticism (punishment)
13. attention
14. praise
    criticize
15. reminders
    reinforced
16. tokens
    reminder (cue)
17. things (tokens)
18. signs (notes)
19. praisers (reinforcers)
20. reinforcement
21. children
22. husband
23. praising

Unit 6 • Exercise 2

This exercise will be used for group discussion during tne next session. No answers are provided here.

Unit 7 • Exercise 1

1. two
2. criticism
3. practice
4. positive
5. communicate
6. care
   teaching
7. reinforcers
8. social
9. descriptive
10. strengthen
11. descriptive
12. descriptive
13. judging
14. less
15. reinforcers (bargaining power)
16. payoff (reward)
17. earned
18. reminder
19. time
20. surprise (treat)
21. reinforce
22. bedtime
23. breakfast
24. bus
25. A
26. time
27. person
28. always
29. praise

Unit 7 • Exercises 2, 3, 4 & 5

These exercises will be used for group discussion during the next session. No answers are provided here. (Answers for Exercise 4 may be found in the Guide for Group Leaders.*)*

Unit 8 • Exercise 1

1. punishers
2. does
3. weakening
4. immediately
5. weakening
6. longer
7. not
8. good
   harmful
9. want
10. avoid
11. stay away
12. move away
13. avoidance
14. escape
15. punishment
16. wrong
17. aggressive (punitive)
18. escape
    fearful
19. hate
20. reduce
21. model
22. immediately
23. reinforcers (rewards)
24. clear cut
25. warning
26. calm (quiet)
27. reinforcement
28. not
29. good
30. safety
31. reinforcements
32. clear cut

Unit 8 • Exercises 2 & 3

These exercises will be used for group discussion during the next session. No answers are provided here. (Answers for Exercise 2 may be found in the Guide for Group Leaders.*)*

Unit 9 • Exercise 1

1. rules
2. after
3. remind
4. remind
5. when
6. conditions (stimuli)
7. red
8. when
9. consequences
10. play
11. tell (inform)
12. him
13. whole
   because
14. general rules
15. example
16. plans
   before
17. fighting (beating up)
18. good manners
   bed
19. more
20. good guest
21. remember
22. consequence
23. enforced
24. teach
25. no
26. yes
27. yes
28. no
29. yes
30. no
31. no
32. yes
33. taught
34. one
35. state the rule (say the rule)
36. correct (right)
37. fade
38. protests

Unit 9 • Exercises 2 & 3

These exercises will be used for group discussion during the next session. No answers are provided here. (Answers for Exercise 2 may be found in the Guide for Group Leaders.*)*

Unit 10 • Exercise 1

This exercise will be used for group discussion during the next session. No answers are provided here. (Answers may be found in the Guide for Group Leaders.*)*